LIFE AFTER DEATH

Don't Let the Enemy/Innerme
Kill You Off!

By D'Antquonese T. Reed

Little Rock, Arkansas

Life After Death: Don't Let the Enemy/Innerme Kill You Off!

Copyright © 2018 By D'Antquonese T. Reed

For inquiries please contact:
ISpeak Publishing Services
http://www.tiffanymooerenterprises.webs.com
Contact the Publisher via email: ISpeakPublish@gmail.com
Contact the Author via email: enemyinnerme2018@gmail.com
All rights reserved. No part of this book may be reproduced, stored in a retrieved system, or transmitted in any form or by any means, electronic, mechanical, photocopying, recording, scanning, or otherwise, without the prior written permission of the author.

All Scriptures come from the New International Standard, Amplified and the King James Version of the Holy Bible unless otherwise indicated.

Disclaimer

All the material contained in this book is provided for educational and informational purposes only. No responsibility can be taken for any results or outcomes resulting from the use of this material.

While every attempt has been made to provide information that is both accurate and effective, the author does not assume any responsibility for the accuracy or use/misuse of this information.

Printed in the United States of America

ISpeak Publishing Service
Little Rock, AR.
501-519-6996

DEDICATION

First and foremost, I want to thank the Lord Almighty for blessing me to be one of His chosen few to write a book ... not just any book, but a book that will inspire, encourage and empower people to surrender to God and allow Him to be Lord over their lives. I pray that someone will read this and come away saying, "What must I do to be saved?" or "What can I do to build a stronger relationship with God?"

God is such an awesome, wonderful God. I mean, He's so AWESOME, I can't really put all my gratitude into words. I try my best, however, to show Him by daily receiving His grace and mercy by faith through Christ Jesus. That's the only reason I am where I am today.

Jesus, I want to say thank You for personally showing me what it means to give up my life for others. You did it, which means so can I! Thank You for leading by example — being about Your Father's business and enduring what You endured for the sake of our unworthy souls. The best lessons I've taken from Your walk are that we really can love past betrayal, past judgement, past the loss of a loved one; and that we can forgive, and pray for, all those who have hurt us. These were once the hardest things for me to do. I'm not a pro at them yet, but I'm striving every day to forgive so that I, too, may be forgiven. Amen.

Holy Spirit, I'm so grateful that Jesus didn't leave us orphaned, but rather, left us such a powerful best friend as You. I want to recognize You every day of my life. I need You like I need oxygen to live. Without You giving me the wisdom daily to do what is asked of me by the Lord God, I know I wouldn't make it. I know I don't always listen to Your advice and direction; I'm so grateful that You never give up on me! Amen.

Wisdom, thank you for seeing something in me that I don't. You always have what I need to overcome fear, doubt and hate toward myself and others. You help me see the good in every situation, especially when I get in my feelings about a thing. I so thank God for you! I need you in my life daily.

To the angels that God has put in charge of me: Thank you for obeying Him and protecting me and my loved ones. I pray you know without a doubt that I'm so grateful to have you. Thank you for fighting demons I can't see and deflecting the weapons that are being formed and shot at me daily. As I think back, I have to thank you for protecting me in situations during my youth that could have been much worse than they were. You are such a blessing.

I want to thank my parents, Paquita and George Reed, for allowing God the opportunity to bless them with a seed such as me. Mama and Daddy, I know I wasn't the easiest child to raise. I understand now that you did the best you could to raise me right. Mama, a lot of things happened to me during my youth that I didn't talk about, nor did I understand why they had to happen to me. After I became an adult, you and I had a chance to talk. I shared with you those things I'd kept to myself, and you said you now understood the reason I acted out the way I did. I personally thank you for your love and understanding, especially after you had a *chance* to understand me. I'm so grateful to God for allowing you and me time to cry, laugh and forgive together before you left this earth on March 15, 2011. I was able to give you your flowers while you were still here. You got a chance to see your prayers answered concerning me. You literally "loved the hell" out of me. I will forever be grateful to you for that. You weren't pleased with all the decisions I made; yet you never disowned me, nor did your love for me waver. Rest in love, Paquita D. Reed. You are forever loved and will always be missed.

I want to thank my grandparents, David and Betty Vann, for being the most AWESOME Grandparents ever. I know I was a handful to deal with. I was so full of energy and curiosity that I constantly wore you out! I thank you, too, for never giving up on me.

- To my grandfather: Thank you for loving my grandmother like no other person on this earth. I'd heard about some of the not-so-good things you had once done. They never mattered to me because of who you were to my grandmother and her daughter, your stepchild. There are not many men left with that degree of character, so to you I say THANK YOU. I never saw you treat her, or us, like we didn't come from your bloodline. You never had any children of your own, yet you loved us as if we were yours. Thank you for always allowing me to be myself, no matter what others said about me. You always encouraged me to be great. You went to be with the Lord July 15, 2018 … exactly seven months and seven days after your beloved wife. Rest in love, David D. Vann.

- Grandmama, what an awesome example of unconditional love you displayed for us to follow! You weren't perfect, yet you were perfect for me. You always saw the good in others. I watched you love those who'd been thrown away by others; those who were looked down on by others. I thank God for giving me such a beautiful example for loving people for who they are with the knowledge that He would complete the work He had begun in them. Those who mistreated you, stole from you or otherwise dishonored you were loved even more by you in return. Thank you for being a wonderful special education teacher for 50-plus years, helping others to see the good in themselves. I love you and your beautiful soul, with which I was blessed until you left this earth Dec. 8, 2017. Rest in love, Betty J. Vann.

To my beautiful children, Re'Jenai Mitchell and Svanti Oaties, who pretty much grew up with me: I love you more than you'll ever know. Thank you for hanging in there. You have always been my motivation for being and doing better every day. I know that your early upbringing wasn't ideal, due to your mama fighting her personal demons and due to your own personal struggles. I thank God that when I invited Him into our lives, things got a lot better. We still had our struggles, yet we had them with God by our side. GLORY!!! Keep finding your way through Christ Jesus. I know that God has you in His hands, so I'm not worried about how your lives will go. Thanks, Re'Jenai, for blessing your mama with two beautiful grandbabies, S'Vannah Cattleya Davis and Stephen Sivad Davis. I also thank God for my five bonus children, as well as my three babies who went to be with the Lord due to miscarriage:

To my godparents, I just want to say thank you so much for always being there for me.

- Delois Riley, you are the greatest mentor anyone could ever ask for. You are an inspiration to many people, especially women, whether or not they let you know. You are a true example of a faith walker. You don't just *talk* it, you *live* what you preach, and I personally thank you for that.

- My dear Papa John (John Riley), you have been the perfect example of a gentle father figure. I'm so thankful to God for sending you to my godmother. God knows exactly what we need, even when we don't have a clue. The love and advice you have given me over the years have helped me to grow into the lady I am now. You've shown me what to expect and accept from a Godly man, just by the way you carry yourself and the way you love and care for your wife. You are an awesome man of God.

I would like to also give a humble, grateful thank-you to my stepmom, Victoria Webb-Reed. From day one, you have been nothing but good to me and my children. When you came into our lives, our family life was a little crazy, and my relationship with my dad hasn't always been the best. Yet I can remember countless times you would step in and allow the Lord to use you to bring about some peace. I know you have your own ups and downs. But you always selflessly try to make sure others, especially family, are OK. We've prayed together and for each other, and I'm more thankful for those moments than you know.

To all the loved ones who have prayed for me, encouraged me to "keep it moving," and loved me through it all — Aunt Lynetta, Pamela Terry, Danette Strons, Angela Henderson, Eshea "Peaches" Davis, Shannta "Taya" Brigham (Rest in Love … gone too soon) and Erikka Williams, to name a few — I'm forever thankful and grateful for you. To my god-sisters, Tanisha and Precious Weatherspoon, you ROCK! I love you all to the moon and back. May God continue to bless you all tremendously. I'm so thankful to Him for placing every single one of you in my life.

ACKNOWLEDGMENTS

To all the people reading this, I'm grateful for you. Thank you for purchasing this book and taking the time to learn what God has put on *my* heart so that it may be a blessing to *your* heart. The Lord God seeks to bless and help us all. Once again, I say that I'm blessed and grateful to be one of the vessels He has chosen to spread His Gospel to the nations. I love all my brothers and sisters in Christ Jesus.

Thank you, Pastor Tiffany Greene-Moorer, for offering your services and your advice on how to articulate my thoughts in book form. Thanks to you and ISpeak Publishing for taking a chance on me, an unknown author with a godly purpose and vision that needs to be shared with the world. I can't say thank you enough. Love you much!

I want to give a special thanks to my photographer, Danette Strons. Thank you for your vision and your love for me, as well as your love for what you do. Love you much. I would also like to give a special thanks to my beautiful, humble editor, Helaine R. Williams, and her ministry, Make It Plain Ministries. Thank you for your time and patience, and for respecting my vision for this book. May God bless you both.

TABLE OF CONTENTS

Dedication iii

Acknowledgments ix

Introduction 1

Chapter One: Overcoming Defeat: Leaning To His
    Understanding 5

Chapter Two: Enduring Your Promised Trials And
    Tribulations 11

Chapter Three: My Favorite Scripture (Matthew 6:33) 28

Chapter Four: Trusting God Is A Must! 35

Chapter Five: Trusting God Is A Journey 42

Chapter Six: Let's Start Together 63

Chapter Seven: How Do You Trust God? 70

Chapter Eight: "How Can I Mature Spiritually?" 77

Chapter Nine: Learning His Perfect Will For Your Life ... 85

Chapter Ten: Trusting God: The Payoff 109

Bibliography 116

INTRODUCTION

Don't let the enemy/innerme kill you off!

What?

Yes, you read that correctly.

If you take a good look at your life, you'll doubtless see that you faced many problems that seemed insurmountable because of that ol' devil himself, or the "inner me" — your own way of thinking/understanding.

Proverbs 3: 5-6 is a Scripture that's familiar to many: *"Trust in the Lord with all thine heart, and lean not unto thine own understanding. In all thy ways acknowledge him, and he shall direct thy paths"* (KJV). Many quote these words but do not abide by them. They ignore the appearance of the word *all* in both verses.

I personally believe that this particular Scripture was meant for everyone. Whether you're a seasoned believer or just learning *how* to believe in Christ Jesus, Proverbs 3:5-6 will keep you from making countless mistakes, especially the same ones over and over. No matter how much the enemy/innerme tries to get you off focus, you need only remember to keep your mind stayed on the things of God, put your trust in Him and let His perfect will work in your life.

Sometimes it may feel or even look like the things you've prayed and fasted for are not going to come to pass. Know this: If you truly put your trust in God and let His perfect will work in your life, He will give you even greater than what you are believing Him for.

I will give you pieces of my life in the pages that follow. As a survivor of a life once consumed by abuse, partying, drugs, unforgiveness and sexual confusion that for a time manifested as a lesbian lifestyle, I'm a firm believer that I can help you make better choices for yourself and your family. After you read about some of the not-so-good choices I've made throughout my life, I pray that you will be encouraged to move forward. I pray that, rather than giving up on yourself, you will allow God to turn your bad moments into good. This book is to let you know that your time in the valley is a testimony for you to share with all who may need to hear it; it's also my aim with this book to help you release that testimony. Don't listen to the enemy/innerme tell you that it would be a big mistake for you to share. The devil is a liar. Sharing your testimony will bless you as well as those with whom you share.

As I share my personal experiences and testimonies, remember that although we may not have the same experiences, Bible Scriptures reveal that we all share similar ones. You'll see that I've been very hard-headed in some areas of my life. But my story is proof that there's still hope after every storm. There's hope for you and your loved ones! Keep fighting the good fight of faith. Keep believing and you will have beauty for your ashes! It's a promise from God in Isaiah 61:3-4: *"To appoint unto them that mourn in Zion, to give unto them beauty for ashes, the oil of joy for mourning, the garment of praise for the spirit of heaviness; that they might be called trees of righteousness, the planting of the Lord, that he might be glorified. And they shall build the old wastes, they shall raise up the former desolations, and they shall repair the waste cities, the desolations of many generations"* (KJV).

I pray that reading about my not-so-good life moments, and my elevation in Christ Jesus despite them, blesses your soul. Feel free to share this book with others. My prayer is that someone will be able to break free from their bondage due to what I've shared under the instructions of the Holy Spirit. God, I pray that You bless every reader with what they need to get from this book.

All right — ready or not, here we go with my testimony. I have refrained from revealing the actual names of some of the people I mention. Otherwise, I haven't sugar-coated any details or held anything back. It's my hope that you can handle it. (Anything I omitted here, I will share in future books.)

Again, we all have times when things just seemed hopeless and we wanted to give up. If you are in the midst of such a time, know that giving up is not an option. Christ Jesus endured ... and so can you. **DON'T LET THE ENEMY/ INNERME KILL YOU OFF!!!**

CHAPTER ONE

Overcoming Defeat: Leaning to His Understanding

It was a beautiful, yet confusing time in my life. The year was 2007. I was just coming out of a life that had, up to that point, been filled with confusion and chaos.

Wait. Let me back up to December 2006, when I brought my fears and my heart to the Lord God — for real this time. You know how we do. We get in a tight spot and ask God to help us, only to return to the same mess after He does. I believe that happens because we hadn't really repented; we'd prayed out of fear rather than sincerity. Can you relate yet? Yes? I'm glad you're being honest with yourself. Anyway, I was serious in December 2006 when I asked God to save me from myself. I didn't want to die in my mess.

In June 2007, the Lord God paid me a visit in my bathroom mirror. He showed me what He saw at that moment in my life. It was totally different from what I saw. See, to be absolutely free from my mess, I had to denounce all fleshly ways of thinking and doing things. I couldn't lean on my own understanding anymore. I had to trust a God I knew only through listening to Big Mama talk about Him and going to the church building every now and then.

This wasn't easy to do, yet it wasn't totally difficult. The Holy Spirit was pulling on me, showing me things. Yet, I didn't want to respond to the call. You know how it is; you don't want to give up the things you had fun doing. For me, that was a lot. I mean a *lot*. When the Lord says in His Word that He "will never leave you nor forsake you," He means it! I know this, because I had been through too many experiences that would have labeled me as "leavable" in the eyes of many.

During the summer of 2006, I was going to the gay clubs quite frequently and getting high on just about every drug you could name. I was so chemically and emotionally messed up, I would just burst out crying anytime, anywhere. I would be in the midst of enjoying myself, then just start boo-hooing. But I'd also be praying.

"Here she goes with this crying mess," my friends would say. One friend/brother at that time, Lord rest his soul, would try to defend me: "She's not playing, y'all, she's for real." The same friend/brother would fuss at me in private. "Heifer, I told you, you don't belong out here," he'd say. "God has need of you." Me being me, I would always have some smart-alecky reply.

In my heart I knew he was right. I've always *felt* that I was different, but I just couldn't see what he seemed to be able to see. I didn't grow up being taught about spiritual gifts and callings. I went to church — and in my head, that was enough. Lord, was I wrong!

This was my real experience with "leaning not to my own understanding." I was out there in the world, but I had been chosen for this life in Christ Jesus. Remember, God doesn't think like us. He'd predestined my life before He placed me in my mother's womb. As some might say, I'd been handpicked by God. Believe me, if it were left up to me at that time in my life, I would still be out there, married to my girlfriend. We'd had an on-again, off-again relationship, but I thought this woman was the one. She'd proposed to me and I'd accepted. Same-sex marriage was not yet legal in Arkansas, where we lived, so we were about to move to a state that allowed it.

I didn't understood why God wanted this ex-gangbanging drughead, living a lesbian lifestyle, on His team. It wasn't until I had that beautiful/scary encounter with His Holy Spirit in June 2007 that I understood. That was when I surrendered. "Since You won't leave me alone, deliver me! I'm tired of these b*****s and these n*****s and this partying lifestyle!" I cried out to Him. It was a challenge: *If You are Who You and others say You are, then deliver me, heal me, and restore me!*

He did just that. Most of my deliverance happened immediately. Of course, deliverance is a process sometimes and in some situations. With His all-knowing self, God used the process to help me to get to better places in my life — spiritually, mentally, emotionally and otherwise — over time. But it was that June 2007 experience that opened the gate of communication with God's Holy Spirit.

Then the journey began.

Trusting God — conditionally

I recall a time I was believing God for a particular situation to change for the better — because, after all, He's God, right? Others had said, "God will change any situation; just pray." I was still a babe in Christ Jesus. I had just really learned how to pray. I was attending noon prayer daily ... my first attempt at following God, dating back to the year 2001. Remember my telling you previously that I had no in-depth teaching about Jesus? You'll get it in a minute (LBVS – Laughing But Very Serious). OK, so here I am praying daily, doing as I was told, yet I hadn't been *taught*. I certainly hadn't been taught that God doesn't go against anyone's free will.

I was praying that He would change my husband at the time. I never prayed for myself; I solely focused on God changing this man and his ways, I wasn't praying about Kingdom matters. I wasn't asking God to show me who I was. I was simply focused on God changing this man and our horrible marriage — the fighting, the cheating, the disrespect. I thought God would change any situation. I didn't take the time to search the Word for myself ... to "study to show myself approved," as 2 Timothy 2:15 tell us to do. Now God is God and He most definitely can and will change things; yet I lacked the understanding that it had to start with me. True change starts with us. We have to seek after God for ourselves. That's the key. In Matthew 6:33, He says, "But seek ye first the kingdom of God, and his righteousness; and all these things shall be added unto you" (KJV). Because I didn't know, let alone understand this, I backslid when things got worse.

After I came back to the Lord in 2007, He showed me that I had *conditionally* loved and trusted Him. The fighting between my husband and me had worsened to the point that one of us was about to go to prison for murdering the other. I had lost hope in God, to whom I had been praying daily about fixing my marriage. I didn't realize that I had *idolized* my marriage and therefore had been loving and trusting God conditionally — "If You do this, God, I'll do that." Sad to say, many people sitting in church today have failed to realize that their love for God is conditional.

There's not a lot of teaching about idolatry, and that's a shame, because I believe it is so needed. There would be a lot fewer hurting and confused believers. Please build your relationship with Christ Jesus strictly on His foundation — not with an "If You'll do this Lord, I'll promise to do this" mentality. Earthly relationships built on false pretenses don't work out. A relationship with God built on false pretenses definitely won't! **DON'T LET THE ENEMY/ INNERME KILL YOU OFF!**

CHAPTER TWO

Enduring Your Promised Trials and Tribulations

The enemy/inner me tries to destroy so many of us at an early age. I was no exception.

Born in Kansas City, MO, I was the eldest of two girls and a boy born to my parents. We moved around a lot, because my parents had an on-again, off-again marriage for 20 years and my father was in and out of trouble with the law. When I was 9, my mother, brother, sister and I were living with my aunt in Oklahoma. It was there that I was molested multiple times by a woman —the sister-in-law of a family member — who had also come to live with my aunt. After these incidents happened, I began holding things in. I didn't tell my mother what this woman did to me until I was an adult.

I was bullied because I was bowlegged and, unlike the other black children I was around, had hair that was long and wavy. I was also ridiculed for being big for my age. (I spent most of my life hating my body. Until age 30, I didn't feel good enough if my hair, clothes and makeup weren't perfect.)

It didn't help that my dad doted on my sister but not on me. I felt attacked or rejected by everyone I wanted to be around, family and all. I became rebellious.

By the time I was 10, we were back in Kansas City and I'd joined a gang. It may surprise you that I was in a gang at that age, but again, I wasn't the average-size 10-year-old. I looked more mature than others my age, big butt and all. Of course, I attracted the wrong kind of attention. A couple of friends' adult uncles tried to force themselves on me. Thank God, neither had a chance to penetrate me. After the attempted rapes, my mother put me on birth control pills. I was six months away from turning 11.

In the gang, I felt like I had a home ... at least at first. We related to each other. And we were bad news! We'd go shoot up the malls. My mother had no idea. But my satisfaction with gang life was short-lived. A fellow gang member, who'd befriended me at first, turned mean on me. Coming from a group-home background, she wanted to show how "bad" she was.

Then came our close encounter with the police. My parents were on the outs again and we were back with my aunt, this time in Kansas City, Kan. The police showed up looking for somebody else. We gang members thought they were looking for us, so we ran. They caught us. *Uh, no, this ain't my life*, I thought as I was placed in the back of that police car. I didn't want to go to jail. Thank God, I was soon let go.

When the leader of our gang was brutally murdered, that was it for me. I saw that as God's way of showing me, "You don't want this."

I was blessed not to have been beaten or killed ... fates people usually suffer when they decide to leave a gang. But my mother, my siblings and I found ourselves in danger for another reason. My dad had gotten busted in Missouri and extradited to Texas to face charges for crimes he'd committed there. While involved in his crimes in Texas, he'd had run afoul of a gang of Cuban. They came looking for us to take their revenge. My uncle borrowed a van belonging to my mother's parents and came to take us to safety in Blytheville, AR, where my grandparents lived. My mother packed up that van, we headed south, and at the age of 11, I began a new life in a new state.

By the time I was in high school, I had a reputation for being mean because I walked around with this ferocious look on my face all the time. That look was my shield. I didn't deal with a lot of people at school; there were maybe one or two others that I spoke to. I got along fine with my teachers. My grades were pretty good. But they began to slip when, at age 16, I started seeing a man who not only turned out to be older than he looked, but also turned out to be married ... and physically abusive to his wife. I never thought to ask him too many questions. All I knew was that here was someone giving me attention, wooing me, giving me the material things I wanted.

He never touched me, but when I told him I didn't want to see him anymore, he began stalking me. When I found out he was married, my mom and I did what we had to do to get him away from me.

By the end of my senior year I was 17, ready to graduate and leave Blytheville. I went on to study at an executive secretarial school in Dallas and started smoking more weed than the law allowed. I sold it, too. Nevertheless, I was making A's and B's.

Ironically, I left the school after officials decided to move it to a rough part of town. Our school took up two floors of a 15-story building. We students had our own apartments, with two people assigned to each. I may have been smoking and selling drugs, but I didn't want to move to the 'hood! I still remember calling my mother and begging, "Mama, don't let them send me off! Come get me! They're about to send me over to where all those crackheads are!" I was pleading for my life!

It was like I was two people. I always had this other side to me that I couldn't fight off. I had to do something against the grain as a sign of toughness. I felt that if I didn't, people wouldn't respect me. That was also my way of keeping people out of my space. I had built up this wall because every time I'd previously allowed people in my space, I'd gotten hurt. I used to always ask God, "Why do I have to go through so much?" Well, I'd brought much on myself. I believed in giving people and situations second chances, third chances and so forth, thinking there would be a change. God had to show me that some of what I went through was due to family/generational curses that were never dealt with. Of course, *somebody* had to deal with them! I was happy to eventually break those curses so that my children and grandchildren wouldn't go through that mess.

I entered my first adult romantic relationship at age 18. It wasn't much of a relationship, really. This was a friend-guy; we were trying to get something going, but I can't really say he was a boyfriend. A pregnancy resulted; unfortunately, that pregnancy ended in miscarriage. Then I found out that this man was going with another woman ... the mother of his child. When his girlfriend approached me and told me everything, we went together to his job and confronted him. Then I left him alone. I wish I had distanced myself just as quickly from the men I encountered afterward.

I soon began seeing another man, and I became pregnant again. This time I successfully gave birth, although my daughter was premature. She came at seven months instead of nine. I was 19.

I stayed four years with my daughter's father. That was four years of mess. I was 22 when we went our separate ways.

I went on to date and marry my first husband, with whom I had my son. Leaving my support system, I moved to Illinois to be with Husband No. 1 … and found myself a battered wife. He became abusive to the point of throwing me down the stairs and stomping me in my stomach. He cheated on me, then attacked me after I found him cheating. There would be times we'd be in the car; I'd just be sitting there minding my business, and he'd get angry about something and swing on me with my babies in the backseat. In one instance, he came after me in his vehicle while I was in mine. Desperate to get away from him, I was driving 70 miles an hour — in reverse. I know the Lord was with me because I never even swerved.

Husband No. 1's grandmother and other family members refused to believe me when I tried to tell them he was abusive; there were never any injuries to my face. He was clever enough not to hit me there. He would always go for my body, then say to his family, "You know I ain't doin' that. My daddy did that to my mama; why would I do that to her?"

One day at my husband's grandmother's house, we got into an argument. He swung at me, missed, and nearly hit his grandmother in the face. I gave her a look. "Aw, but you said [he] doesn't hit women, huh?" I said before walking out. I respected my elders and didn't want to dishonor my grandmother-in-law by going off on her in her house. But his family had disrespected me by refusing to believe me.

I wasn't the only one who suffered from my husband's temper. On one occasion his physical abuse extended to my daughter, who he disliked. He beat her, supposedly punishing her for some offense, and left a long, nasty mark on her arm.

Things got so bad that I once took half a bottle of prescription pills, trying to end it all. God wasn't ready for me to go.

I attended a church at the time, but it was of a denomination that taught me only to pray, speak in tongues and stay in a bad marriage. That wasn't about to work for me.

In 2003 — when my daughter was 6, my son was nearly 3 — I finally got up enough courage to leave my husband. The day I tried to do so, he attacked me and tried to kill me. I grabbed a little hammer that my friend's mother had given me to defend myself with, and I hit him upside his head with it. The fight ended with both of us going to jail that night.

Now I had called the police on this man a number of times during our marriage. Because of loopholes in the law in Illinois, they always told me they could do nothing. Here I was this night, bleeding profusely from my eye, where he'd broken a blood vessel. However, I was close to being charged with attempted murder because I was an inch away from smashing into his temple with the hammer, which they said would have killed him. I didn't know where the blows were falling; I was just defending myself. If it weren't for God sending my husband's uncle down the hill to our home that particular night, my husband would have been dead and I would have been in prison, possibly for the rest of my life.

My marriage to Husband No. 1 lasted two and a half years. I left him in August 2003; we finally divorced in 2008.

After I left him, I spent the next four years popping pills and smoking weed. I also entered into a same-sex relationship that lasted from 2004 to 2007 and partied at strip clubs and gay clubs with my girlfriend. I knew this relationship was wrong, but that's what I wanted to do at the time. This is how I know God has patience with me.

One thing I can say: I made sure my children were safe, and I didn't expose them to my lifestyle. I never partied in front of them. Whenever I chose to do something I didn't want them to witness, I went to someone else's home. My girlfriend and I didn't display any affection in front of my children. They didn't even realize I was dating her until shortly before we broke up, and that was only because somebody with whom my son got into an argument at school told him.

A couple of months after my breakup with my girlfriend, here came Husband No. 2. He said he'd been watching me and wanted to show me how "real men" handled their business. Of course, I allowed him to slide on into my children's and my lives.

Let me say first off that there were some good things that emerged from my having met Husband No. 2. God had given me the gift of prophecy. It was a gift I'd had all my life, and it was strong. Of course, I'd gone all those years not knowing it for what it was. Husband No. 2, who had a powerful prophetic gift, helped me to recognize and cultivate mine. God also used him to help me cultivate my gift of tongues. He even helped me repair my relationships with my children, with whom I'd inevitably missed some things as I'd partied. I believe this man was meant to be a spiritual mentor and nothing more. Unfortunately, romance got in the way. And, unfortunately, he used his God-given gift as a way to manipulate people. The Word talks about "gifts without repentance," or as the New Living Translation puts it, *"For God's gifts and his call can never be withdrawn"* (Romans 11:29). God doesn't take back His gifts even if the recipients act like monkeys.

I had no idea that Husband No. 2 also had a serious problem with drug addiction. Signs of it, and the resulting demonic oppression, began to manifest once we got married. When he got high, these spirits would have a field day with him Those things were ugly — and I have witnesses to attest to that. They would growl and jump at me. God had to show me how to do some serious spiritual warfare.

Still, I tried to save the marriage. My husband would disappear for weeks or months at a time. I sometimes went to the fleabag crack motels he frequented, honking the car horn and beating on doors to get him to come home. And through all this, I honored him. God would reveal to me that my husband was about to come home from one of his crack binges, then put it on my heart to have a dinner plate ready and a warm bath drawn. I'd be like, "What, Lord?" My pastor at that time also advised me to do this. (Since those days, Husband No. 2 has testified in church about how I would come to the door and welcome him in, with a plate of food on the table, the bathwater ready and his clothes laid out on the side of the bed.)

I even anointed his shoes with oil and prayed over them. I thought all that was crazy, but I made sure I was the vessel through which God worked as He tried to get through to this man. It's unfortunate that my husband kept choosing the wrong path. God can do anything, but He also gives us free will and allows us to make our own choices.

In addition to choosing to abuse drugs, my husband chose to cheat on me. I remember walking down the hallway, my children in their rooms, and eavesdropping on his phone conversations with his sister. At least he *started out* talking to her. When he lowered his voice and began to sound more romantic, I knew something was up. Mind you, he was on my phone! But I didn't confront him.

When he decided to leave me, his sister — who'd been aiding and abetting his girlfriend — came with her to pick him up. "Whenever y'all come get me, I'll be ready, 'cause she's crazy," he told them on the phone before they showed up.

(I didn't know at the time that the woman with my sister-in-law was my husband's mistress. But I'd had a prophetic dream about the woman, down to her build, her skin color and even the curtains in her windows.)

A month and a half after Husband No 2 left, his sister called me, saying I needed to come and get him.

"Hold on. Let me tell you something," I told her. "You and your devils [referring to spirits] came to *my* place of residence and got *my* husband, your brother, who you lied for. So now you keep him."

I did take him back about four months later. But once again he chose another woman over me, driving this woman's truck and even letting my children see him with her. I knew it was the end of the marriage.

We had gotten married May 10, 2008. We divorced two years, three months later – Aug. 10, 2010. In December of that year, he tried to get me to take him back. I refused.

I didn't get bitter, nor did I backslide. By that time, I was more knowledgeable about who God was and how He was working in me and through me.

I continued to grow in the Lord and grow closer to my mother, for which I am so grateful. God had me to give her a word about the physical relations she had been having with the man she was seeing. I told her God didn't want her to die in her sins. After hearing the same word from one of her friends, my mother took it to heart. She and her boyfriend married Jan. 11, 2011. Two months later, her husband found her on the floor. She had passed away of a pulmonary embolism. I went through my grief period, then in August of that year I moved to Texas.

I had been celibate four years when Husband No. 3 came along. He and I had known each other years earlier and had nearly married, but I'd called it off. He and I had begun seeing each other shortly after the first of my two breakups with the girlfriend (the second and final breakup with her being in 2007, when I met Husband No. 2). This time, the engagement to Husband No 3 culminated in our 2014 wedding.

Unfortunately, I didn't realize he was still struggling with alcoholism, an issue that had manifested the first time we'd been together. He was a functional alcoholic; he was able to hold down a job. But alcoholic he was, and it got ugly. He would spend weekends at his mom's house, claiming he was too drunk or hung over to come home. Sometimes I'd go over there to find him knocked out.

"If you want to sip, you can do it at home," I told him. "You don't have to go over there. Matter of fact, your mom is wrong too. If I were a mother-in-law, I wouldn't let my son come and lay up at my house when he has a wife at home." This put a wedge between his mother and me for a while. What type of mother enabled her son like that?

Husband No. 3 and I divorced in 2016. Afterward I traveled and performed in gospel plays. But then Husband No. 2 re-emerged, wanting yet another chance. I began to entertain his conversation. He went so far as to apologize publicly for doing me wrong. That made my heart do a little something! I loved my other husbands, but I was *in love* with Husband No. 2.

This is where my story gets a bit convoluted. I resisted Husband No. 2 at that point; instead I reunited with Husband No. 3. We remarried, then split up again. I eventually *did* go back to Husband No. 2, remarrying him in July 2017. I left only 18 days later after seeing those old demons in his life begin to re-rear their ugly heads. Our second divorce became final in September 2017.

And, believe it or not, I married Husband No. 3 a third time … and divorced him a third time. Yes, I've been through six marriages with three men!

The third time I married Husband No. 3, he was near death. His substance abuse had gone on to include cocaine. I didn't know about this. I just heard the Holy Spirit say, "Reach out to him." I did, and in fact, I apologized to him for my own bratty behavior the other times we'd been together. I was only supposed to *get matters right with him* at that point, not remarry him. In January 2018, right before our third wedding, I clearly heard the Holy Spirit say, "Not right now." But I had already sent out the invitations, so I disobeyed.

I'd spent a lifetime doing what I wanted instead of what God wanted, even after my relationship with God began to strengthen. I could have been so much farther along in my spiritual walk by now. I should have put out a book long before now. God showed me years ago that I had books — as well as music CDs — in me. (I actually sing with a gospel group, Patrick Bean & Bonafide Worshippers; we put a CD out and won an award for it.) I'm just so glad that God is such a loving, forgiving and *patient* God! I'm so grateful that He has given me more time to start releasing books.

When my grandfather died, I felt that all my support system was gone. But then, I heard God tell me to start enjoying my life. *How can I enjoy my life?* I wondered. *Yes, I have my inheritance. I've got a house, I've got a car, I've got money in the bank. I'm set for a pretty good while if I do things right. But how can I enjoy my life?* I struggled with grief for some months. I just wanted to get drunk.

Matter of fact, I puffed a couple puffs of weed, from which I'd been delivered for 11 years. After I took those puffs, God said, "OK, go on. Die."

My chest started to close in and I coughed like there was no tomorrow.

"Don't touch it anymore," God said.

"You don't have to worry, Lord," I replied.

I let go and let God. And let me tell you: When He comes and gives you a double portion of peace and joy after you've been under attack for so long, there's nothing like it!

Ordained by God, or ordained by me?

I hit quite a few bumps in the road that I call my life. Some were God-ordained moments; some were D'Antquonese-made moments. I had to learn the difference between the two.

We've all had these experiences. Some of us are still bumping our heads over the consequences of our self-made mistakes, thinking God has caused our suffering! I was one of those people. I'd be in a relationship that I had no business in and, instead of leaving, I'd say, "I'm waiting on God to bring me out." That sounds familiar, doesn't it? Because of my own lust and my lack of knowledge and maturity, I remained in numerous toxic relationships.

Then, as a babe in Christ, I'd wait for God to extricate me from my pit. Mind you, He had already freed me. Yet — because I was unlearned and failed to obey the Holy Spirit — I remained in bondage. I stayed bound to the belittling comments: I wasn't cute enough. I wasn't small enough. I wasn't smart enough. I was never enough to be honored. Yet, I was "enough" to get sex from, by consent or by marital rape. I was "enough" to impregnate and have a child with. I was "enough" to be a punching bag. I was "enough" to be cheated on.

During my marriage to Husband No 1, I was told, "It'll get better. Keep praying." I prayed. And I got my answer from the Holy Spirit: *Go*. Yet, I stayed ... beaten down, fearful, and unlearned when it came to self-love. I was under the impression that I had to take this treatment; that things would eventually get better. I was told this by women of God. I lacked a strong personal relationship with God, so I listened to them. I would like to tell you that I soon "got it" as I grew further in Christ. No. It took me almost going to prison for 15-plus years after my husband attacked me for trying to leave him.

Even then, I didn't get it. I didn't understand that I put myself in that situation. I was packing to leave him when he called and asked me to come by the dope house to see him. "I want to talk to you real quick," he said. I always sensed when drama or violence was about to take place, and I did in this case. But I just couldn't pull myself away. I feared I wouldn't find anybody else to love me – a woman with two children. I assumed I wasn't good enough for God's best. I didn't realize that this assumption was a lie straight from hell.

So, after our fight and my arrest on suspicion of attempted murder, I found myself sitting on a hard, cold concrete jail floor, pleading with God all night long to get me out of this dysfunctional mess. It took landing in jail, not knowing the outcome of that situation, to drive home the realization that I didn't want this kind of life anymore ... not for myself, and definitely not for my two beautiful children. My daughter, being the eldest, had witnessed the most, and it finally registered that I was a poor example for her. She'd seen that it was acceptable to get hit for speaking her mind. She'd seen that it was acceptable for her to be thrown down a flight of stairs and kicked in the stomach by a husband who didn't want any more babies. What was I thinking? Clearly, I wasn't thinking at all.

But I still had the nerve to be angry at God — the same merciful God Who delivered me from jail with no charges pending. I was still under the impression that God was supposed to fix my marriage. I know, right? Yet, that was my hope. I had seen God restore the marriage of another couple, and I wanted restoration for mine. What I didn't know was that the other couple were *in agreement*. The husband and wife *both* wanted things to change in their marriage. That's the key to the improvement of any relationship between two people — they both have to want it! I had to find out the hard way that this marriage wasn't God's perfect will for my life. Yet, God caused it to work out for my good. God loves us so much that even when we get mad and blame Him for our foolish and fleshly decisions, He turns things around for our good and His glory! Won't He do it? Yes, He will!

My advice to anyone going through a tough/confusing/scary time is to stay prayerful and ask God for His wisdom, knowledge, and understanding. He will give it to you. You just have to remember to do one thing: Obey. **DON'T LET THE ENEMY/INNERME KILL YOU OFF!**

CHAPTER THREE

My Favorite Scripture
(Matthew 6:33)

"*But seek ye first the kingdom of God, and his righteousness, and all these things shall be added unto you,*" according to the King James Version of my favorite Scripture.

Why is that so difficult for so many of us, even when we are shown the dismal consequences of seeking our own false kingdoms — or those of others — first? I'm a textbook case of what can happen when one chooses to do the latter.

You know by what I've written previously that it took me a while to get to where I am now spiritually. I knew what to do, yet for one reason or another I decided my way was better than God's way. My attitude was that God had made a mistake with His decision making concerning my life … especially when my life wasn't going the way I assumed it would. That was my fault for assuming *anything* — my stinkin' thinkin'. I realize that now.

When I decided to come back to the Lord in June 2007, I was spiritually thirsty and therefore serious about our relationship. I gave the Holy Spirit free range in all aspects of my life, even when it came to choosing what I would wear on a given day, underwear included. Yes, I said underwear! Those who knew me during my wild days knew that underwear was something I *didn't* include in my daily wardrobe! (Yes, I'm being *that* honest, and don't act like you've never "gone commando." Even if you haven't, I'll bet you know someone who has, or does.) Anyway, that's how serious I was about my new life in Christ Jesus. I was coming out of that awful darkness into God's marvelous light.

I should have *stuck* with seeking God first.

Allow me to fast-forward a bit. Still a babe in Christ, I began dating Husband No. 2, whom God had blessed with the gift of prophecy. As I previously stated, he did share his gift with me, teaching me how to get in the face of God through the Holy Spirit.

But I was in a vulnerable state. I was seeking after God and the enemy knew it. And he didn't like the fact that I had just come out of his territory after having been one of his best workers. I had no idea, when I was out in the world, that I was anointed by God. But the enemy knew it. That's why he'd tried his best to keep me out there. When I finally lay hold of God and was learning about His purpose for my children's and my lives — well, here came Slewfoot, as my grandma called him. And he was going to try his best to destroy me.

Husband No. 2 knew what to say, how to say it, and when to say it, and my children and I thought he was the one. The Lord God sent me signs to the contrary, especially when I went on my first fast. As you know, I didn't listen. I was just hard-headed, as the old folks used to say.

I thought the enemy was angry *because* this man and I were together. Husband No. 2 was so different ... so anointed. Earlier I'd mentioned Romans 11:29, which says that God doesn't take back the gifts He gives us, even if we misuse or neglect them. Believe me – Husband No. 2 was operating in his gift, but he wasn't living according to God's will for his life. As I stated before, I was still a babe learning about all this. Some of the things he said and did should have bothered me. Had I listened to what I know now to be the Holy Spirit, I would never have ended up putting that man, that relationship, before God. You would think I'd have been a little wiser from dealing with my first husband and those spirits. But from that time to this, I'd backslidden for four years and had taken on even *more* bad spirits ... spirits I had to fight off with the help of the Lord. What little spiritual knowledge I'd gained in years prior were covered up in mess. I couldn't see or hear as clearly as I would have been able to do had I stayed with God after I left that first toxic marriage. As a result, I went through the ringer again. Husband No. 2 had many demons and the enemy clearly wanted to take us both down. All hell broke loose in my children's and my lives. More so mine. How many know that there's just so much we mothers are going to allow our children to endure, especially if we can help it?

The trouble began shortly after we started getting serious. (Truth be told, it could have already been going on; I just didn't have any proof.) His babymama started tripping. He started to get in trouble. Then all types of stuff started hitting the fan. He cheated on me with other women and a man. Oops, did I write that? Yes, I did. Of course, he denied being with this man. Dude was lying on him, he claimed.

By now, however, I was seriously involved with this man. So yes, I kept going with him; again, I thought things would miraculously get better once the devil left us alone. And again, I just wanted some form of love.

I was hearing the Holy Spirit well. But I was second-guessing what I heard. I put this "all-knowing man of God's" words above the Lord's, and I had no idea of the power that God had placed in me. I should have been paying more attention, because I had fasted and prayed for God's power and the spirit of discernment — and oh, did He bless me with just that! I thought my boyfriend was the one God was using because he still flowed in his gift of prophecy. The Holy Spirit had been trying to show me that He had filled *me* with His power, yet I overlooked it. I was paying no attention to Romans 11:29; nor was I paying any attention to 2 Timothy 3:5, where the Apostle Paul writes *about "having a form of godliness, but denying the power thereof."* This verse tells us that *"from such* [we should] *turn away"* (KJV).

I not only didn't turn away, I married the man. You are probably thinking, *This girl must be desperate or crazy*. I think I was a little bit of both! I didn't realize it was the innerme, my lust for this man, that caused me to go after him and stay with him, even after the warning signs were presented. What I needed to learn from him, I had already gotten. Yet I wanted him to be my partner, thinking I could help change him. How many of us know now that we can't change anybody, especially someone who is clearly OK with being the way they are?

God was using me to help many other people. *Surely*, I thought, *God is going to help with me with my man*. I had to realize one important thing: God's not going to go against anyone's will. I blame myself for failing to listen to the Lord and apply what I had previously learned.

Let me fast forward again to when I started writing this book. My life was already somewhat in an unsettled state due to my losing one of the loves of my life, my dear grandmother, in December of 2017. I started writing this book in January 2018. At that time God had placed me in the position of caregiver for my grandfather. He stayed about three hours from me at that time. God knows I enjoyed every moment of that role. I wouldn't trade it for anything in this world.

I was also engaged to Husband No. 3 for the third time. In March 2018, we tied the knot once again in a beautiful, sports-themed wedding. The marriage began getting rough not even two weeks afterward. I found out later that my husband didn't really *want* to remarry me; yet, he never said a mumbling word.

I'll fast-forward once again, this time to the end of June 2018. I had just left a banking job and gone to Texas for what was supposed to be a two-week vacation. It was cut to a week, due to my grandfather getting ill and being admitted to the hospital only six months after my grandmother's passing. The doctors thought his intestines had ruptured. The whole time he was in the hospital, he kept telling the staff he was OK, that they weren't going to find anything wrong, but that he was ready to go home. He was mentally preparing to be with his Father God, his wife, and his daughter.

Sure enough, to the surprise of the hospital staff, my grandfather was found to be suffering only from serious scar tissue from a previous surgery. But, again, he was ready to go. He spent two and a half weeks in the hospital, then spent his last five days in hospice.

During this time, I had no support from Husband No. 3. He went on a drinking binge that kept him away for about a week and a half. Of course, that was the last straw. This man had given my grandfather his word that he would be there for me and help me do what was needed. That turned out to be a lie. And I was already dealing with other issues, including family drama.

"Lord, I don't understand why You want me to endure this pain, yet I trust You," I prayed.

After I buried my grandfather, I filed for divorce and proceeded with my life. That's when I heard God saying, "Start enjoying your life." My grandfather told me the same thing before he got to the point of being unable to talk anymore. Thanks to Him, I'm doing just that.

After all the adversity that has taken place in my life — to the point where I had at one point given up on finishing this book — I still thank God! I thank God for the time He gave me with my grandfather for those two and a half weeks. I also thank Him for allowing me to be a wife to Husband No. 3 for a time, even though I don't understand everything about that situation. I pray that whatever God needed His son to get while being married to me, he got. I grew quite a bit just from going through this chapter of my life. I don't regret the love and recognition I gave him while we were married. I pray that God blesses the journey he has chosen to take without me. God knows best.

If you didn't get anything else from my testimony, please remember this: Keep Matthew 6:33 first in your life, especially when it comes to decision making. Don't just do it because I say so; it's the Word of God. God's Word will truly keep us. The thing is, you must want to be kept! **DON'T LET THE ENEMY/INNERME KILL YOU OFF!**

CHAPTER FOUR

Trusting God is a Must!

Much of the struggling we do as believers comes because we fail to trust God. And the Bible has plenty to say about the importance of trusting in God:

"But I have trusted in thy mercy; my heart shall rejoice in thy salvation." (Psalm 13:5, KJV)

"Some trust in chariots, and some in horses: but we will remember the name of the Lord our God." (Psalm 20:7, KJV)

"Oh Lord of hosts, blessed is the man that trusteth in thee." (Psalm 84:12, KJV)

"The king was overjoyed and ordered that Daniel be lifted from the den. Not a scratch was found on him, for he had trusted in his God" (Daniel 6:23, NLT). The Jews were at this time under the rule of the Medes, ruled over by King Darius. Darius favored Daniel — who was a great administrator — enough to put him in charge of his whole empire, but Daniel had his haters among the king's other top officials. These haters tricked the king into establishing a 30-day rule that anybody who prayed to any being other than him would be thrown

into a den of hungry lions. Daniel of course disobeyed, and the king had no choice but to carry out the punishment. Daniel's trust in God shut up the lions' mouths!

"I pray that God, the source of hope, will fill you completely with joy and peace because you trust in him. Then you will overflow with confident hope through the power of the Holy Spirit" (Romans 15:13, NLT)

And of course, there's the Scripture I already quoted, Proverbs 3:5-6.

I had many lessons in trust. Some were obviously major. Other lessons weren't so dramatic, but they were no less profound.

One trust lesson I had to learn came with my first experience with fasting. The concept of fasting was new to me; growing up, I had not heard any teaching about it. But I was spiritually thirsty ... very thirsty. I was going through my transformation. I no longer wanted the liquor; I no longer wanted the weed; I didn't want *anything* to do with my old way of living. The Lord snatched all my old desires from me when I came back home to Him.

For those who haven't experienced immediate deliverance, it's possible; I'm a living witness. Yet, Matthew 17:17-21 tells us that certain things only come about by fasting and praying:

> **Then Jesus answered and said O faithless and perverse generation, how long shall I be with you? How**

> long shall I suffer you? bring him hither to me. And Jesus rebuked the devil; and he departed out of him; and the child was cured from that very hour. Then came the disciples to Jesus apart, and said, Why could not we cast him out? And Jesus said unto them, Because of your unbelief; for verily I say unto you, If ye have faith as a grain of mustard seed, ye shall say unto this mountain, Remove hence to yonder place; and it shall remove; and nothing shall be impossible until you. Howbeit this kind goeth not out but by prayer and fasting. (KJV)

(It's very important to read and apply this Scripture to your life, as well as the lives of those you're praying for so that they, too, may experience true deliverance.)

As I said, God snatched pretty much everything from me. Yet, there's this spirit called Residue. It's real, y'all. So, I needed some prayer and fasting to get rid of that spirit.

The Holy Spirit had me watching Trinity Broadcasting Network (TBN) and, of course, reading and studying the Word of God. On one particular beautiful day in January 2008, I saw a pastor by the name of Jentezen Franklin on TBN. He caught my attention because, like me, he's loud and gets very excited! He began talking about this corporate fast that he and those in his ministry were about to start. Anyone was welcome to join, he said; all you needed was faith. "Yeah, you watching on TBN," he added. Now, that about freaked me all the way out! Seriously, I had never experienced anything like that. I had just gone unto the Lord God and inquired about doing my first fast, then this. Bam!

I eventually calmed down and continued to listen to Pastor Franklin, because I had been praying about getting rid of my residue. I wanted freedom ... the kind of freedom that Jesus told the people about in John 8:33-36:

> **They answered him, We be Abraham's seed, and were never in bondage to any man; how sayest thou, Ye shall be made free? Jesus answered them, Verily, verily, I say unto you, Whosoever committeth sin is the servant of sin. And the servant abideth not in the house for ever: but the Son abideth ever. If the Son therefore shall make you free, ye shall be free indeed. (KJV)**

When Pastor Franklin said the fast would be for 21 days, however, my mouth literally dropped! "He must be tripping!" I said to the Lord. "I have never been on a fast! And you want me, D'Antquonese, to fast for *21 days*? I knew God wanted me to fast for my betterment. Yet I was like, "Why can't we start small, Lord? One to three days would have been just fine with me, but *21 days, Lord?*"

I was in panic mode! But the Holy Spirit quickly calmed me down and assured me that I could do this — with His help, of course. I had a lot going on at that time (my life story).

I didn't realize that I was in a place where God was accelerating my progress. I needed to catch up in the spirit realm.

So, I was trying to see how I was about to do this. The Holy Spirit reassured me that He had me; I just needed to trust Him. What I thought would be extremely difficult, wasn't difficult at all. It wasn't the *easiest* thing to do, but I had to start somewhere. This is where my "trusting God is a must" journey began! It taught me about discipline and dedication.

I have another journey in this same category that I believe will bless someone. After I share this next experience in trust, I'll leave you be ... until the next book.

I was walking through my dark-valley experience with Husband No. 2, and I'd had just about enough. I had been helping him fight all type of demons, mainly crack cocaine, and it had taken its toll on me. One day, I went over to my godmother's apartment to just get away and to vent. The next thing I knew, there was a knock at the door. It was my husband. Oh, I was heated! *Why in the hell is he here?* I asked myself. *This was my moment to get free.* So much for that! God had another plan.

My godmother, being no respecter of persons, let my husband in. That's why I love this woman so much — she loves everybody and tries to help people all she can. It's funny now, but it wasn't funny then. I just didn't want this man around. Again, I was *heated*. And I got into an argument with my husband. My godmother tried to intervene and diffuse the argument, telling me to shut up and listen. But I kept interrupting her with my angry outbursts. My blood was boiling, especially as my husband had begun laughing at her attempts to calm me. I didn't see anything funny, honey. I knew I wasn't going to disrespect my godmother in her house, but I sure wanted to hit my husband one good time!

When one of my godmother's young granddaughters stopped by, I saw a means of escape from the situation. I asked the child to take a walk with me and she agreed to do so. We left the house and walked to a park. Baby Girl wanted to do something — I can't remember what – and I told her no. She began to whine. Normally this isn't how she acts, so I told her to stop acting like a baby. "You should realize that if I said no, it's for your own good," I told her.

Then the Holy Spirit dealt with me.

"Now do you see how you were acting?" He asked.

"No," I answered, pouting of course.

"You were acting like a whining child, instead of listening to me."

I had to repent. "Wow. I'm so sorry, Lord. I didn't see it that way … nor was I trying to at that moment."

I was too busy trying to make my point instead of listening to the wisdom that God was trying to impart to me through my godmother. I got all self-righteous and defensive, when all I had to do was listen.

I've already given a few Scriptures on trust. In case I didn't convince you, look at Jeremiah 17:5-8.

> This is what the Lord says: "Cursed are those who put their trust in mere humans, who rely on human strength and turn their hearts away from the Lord. They are like stunted shrubs in the desert, with no hope for the future. They will live in the barren wilderness, in an uninhabited salty land. But blessed are those who trust in the Lord and have made the Lord their hope and confidence. They are like trees planted along a riverbank, with roots that reach deep into the water. Such trees are not bothered by the heat or worried by long months of drought. Their leaves stay green, and they never stop producing fruit."
> (NLT)

The last thing the enemy/innerme wants us is rooted, grounded, at peace, joyful and blessed. He wants us confused, tormented, fearful and depressed, so he'll catch us at our vulnerable times — as early as our childhood; he plays dirty — and put one over on us. Unfortunately, some of us believers don't catch on. Study these Scriptures on trust. Be doers, not just hearers (or readers) of the Word. Watch the benefits begin to manifest. God doesn't promise us easy lives, but He will keep us strengthened and steadied as he walks us through our valleys. **DON'T LET THE ENEMY/ INNERME KILL YOU OFF!**

CHAPTER FIVE

Trusting God is a Journey

I was watching TBN again. That's all I ever watched at the time; I didn't want anything else tainting my spirit. I was very serious about my new beginning, and I was going to continue this journey no matter what it cost me. If it meant giving up my favorite shows on Black Entertainment Television as well as my murder-mystery shows, so be it. I knew I had to do it! I was going to get my life in order, *with* some order. Sometimes, I'd watch Little Rock, AR-based television station KTVN, known as VTN, which is another good inspirational station. I allowed my children to watch only the Disney and Nickelodeon channels.

I know some of you are probably saying, "It doesn't take all that." Well, for me it did. I knew what I could handle and what I couldn't. I was determined to learn self-control ... a very important thing to do when you're serious about changing your life. Even now, there are certain things I don't watch because they bother my spirit. What bothers me may not bother you. I urge you to be honest with yourself and put away whatever you know you need to stop letting into your eye gates and ear gates. Everything is not meant to go into your spirit once you've decided to embark on a journey of changing for the better spiritually. Make sure you find what works for you and stick with it. If you fall, get back up and keep it moving.

Anyway, I was watching TBN again not long after I'd finished my 21-day fast. The pastor whose show I was watching encouraged viewers to get involved in a local church. I kind of cringed and said, "I'm good on that," because some of my past church experiences had not so good. Yet, I knew God was tugging at me. He reminded me of a time when I was deep in my worldly mess and still taking my butt to church! I even took my girlfriend to church when I was living a lesbian lifestyle! Even then, I knew I needed God. And now I had the nerve to act like I didn't want to go church. At this point in my life, I was cool with watching my TV church ministries. Hey, they were helping me — right? Yet, God wanted me to go further. He had need of me in an actual sanctuary, fellowshipping with other believers.

I wanted to obey God and assemble myself with other believers; I was just over the whole religious thing. I knew in my heart of hearts that there was definitely more to being a believer in Christ Jesus than the religious aspect. But I decided to trust God again. I was a little scared, but I was going to obey.

I prayed first. I wasn't going to make the mistake of just going to any church. In the past I wasn't that wise, and things took place that could have turned me away from God for good. That's another reason I praise God the way I do. He didn't allow my soul to die out there like that. Hallelujah!

Because I allowed the Holy Spirit to lead me to the church He wanted me to attend, I had an awesome experience. I fellowshipped with other believers who truly taught the Bible. The church also had noonday prayer service, which was something I was familiar with and liked participating in. I chose to trust the Lord again, and it paid off.

This was an experience that moved me further in my dedication to Christ Jesus, my discipline, and my submission to those who have rule over me. The Lord revealed to me that if I was mistreated by leaders or fellow believers in the future, I shouldn't simply abandon Him and backslide, as I had before. Rather, I should allow Him to show me how to pray for these saints, and He would deal with them accordingly. That's when I learned more about Hebrews 13:17: *"Obey them that have the rule over you, and submit yourselves: for they watch for your souls, as they that must give account, that they may do it with joy, and not with grief: for that is unprofitable for you"* (KJV)

I know it can be difficult to trust people. I've been in that place before, and to be truthful, I *still* get in that place when I'm experiencing something new. I get a little fearful, which is normal because we're human. If this happens to you, just remember not to stay in that place for too long. That's where the enemy/innerme begins to play with your mind. Your best defense is to trust God and renew your mind daily, yielding to the things of God.

Trusting God is the best decision I've ever made. It can be the same for you. You need only allow yourself to be vulnerable unto the Holy Spirit. He'll walk with you every step of your life journey. Once you try God and see that He's faithful at just being Him, you'll never want to turn away from Him again. I'm not saying you won't ever have those moments where you want to just give up and throw in the towel. I'd be lying. It's that pull from within (the Holy Spirit) that will bring you back to your senses and help you go a little further. Then, you'll fully understand why God says in several Scriptures, including Hebrews 13:5, that He will never leave you nor forsake you. You'll also understand why we are told in Psalm 118:8 that it's better to trust in the Lord than in man.

Even with this knowledge, we'll still trust family members and so-called friends. That's like asking for disaster to happen! (This kind of thing will continue if we haven't prayed and asked God to show us who to confide in.) Yet, we have the nerve to get mad at the person who betrayed our trust, and sometimes even get mad at God. It's our own fault for not listening to the voice of the Holy Spirit! I'm not saying we can't have faith in a person. I'm saying that we need to ask for spiritual discernment concerning everybody ... even ourselves, because yes, our own minds can deceive us.

If you're not doing so already, ask the Holy Spirit to reveal those with whom you can share details of your life.

Know this one thing for sure: You'll ALWAYS be able to trust in the God Who gave you life. He let us know in John 15:16; that He chose us; we didn't choose Him. Go read this Scripture and get the full revelation of what's He's saying to you. Our Father God wants to talk and sup with you. God doesn't care where you've been, nor where you are right now in life; He always has time for His child. He's just waiting on you ... yes, seriously, it's that easy.

Start by having a regular conversation with Him as if you're talking to someone for whom you have mad respect or would normally share your life with. Talking to God like that is going to elevate you to new realms. Not only does He listen, He responds! I promise you that I fall more in love with God daily, especially when I'm going through my toughest battles. He just lets me have my temper tantrums and pity parties. Then He'll ask me, "Are you finished?" When I surrender those emotions to Him, the Holy Spirit comes right in, comforts me and gets my mind, heart, and soul back on track. God then tells me to get back up and be of good courage because He's ALWAYS with me and He ALWAYS has my back. That is the most real thing I've known. God has proven Himself over and over again.

The bottom line: Always trust God. **DON'T LET THE ENEMY/INNERME KILL YOU OFF!**

I'd like to share with you the story of Job. I pray that it will help you understand a little bit more why I say that trusting God is a must.

Job, the subject of his own book in the Old Testament, caught my eye due to the simple fact that this devout man went through so much and *continued to stand* on the things of God. Despite Job's fierce devotion to God, the enemy was allowed by God to test Job's faith to the max! "Why him?" some may ask. How many of you can actually say that if you lost everything — your family, your wealth — you'd continue to hold fast to the God Who allowed these things to happen to you? What if, to add insult to injury, you were struck with painful boils all over your body? What if your spouse, who you dearly love, urges you to "curse God and die"?

Let's be real: Few would survive Job's trials. Perhaps those who have already been through trials and tribulations, and benefited from their faithfulness to God, would survive. But those who are still babes in Christ, like I was when I first read Job's story, can't begin to fathom their survival. Well, maybe I was the only one who felt that way! Babyyyy, I was like, "Lord, I don't know about this one!" (LOL). We might as well be totally honest with ourselves and God!

As we go down this path that is Job's story, I want you to begin to put yourself in his shoes. As you do, you'll see that most of us have experienced a little self-righteousness in our pain, as he did. Yes, Job had a little self-righteousness going on … just as we all do, at some time or another, throughout our walk with Jesus.

Here's an example. I was going through a dark-valley experience in my life. At that time, I felt like I shouldn't be going through this. By then, I was doing exactly what was asked of me by the Holy Spirit. I was tithing faithfully. I was assembling myself with brothers and sisters in the Gospel. So yes, I felt very self-righteous. What I didn't know was that my tribulation didn't have anything to do with me. God was allowing this to happen to me because He had a far greater plan in mind. See, our dark-valley experiences are designed to make us stronger in every area of our lives. God also uses our experiences and resulting testimonies to encourage others going through similar or worse problems: *If Brother or Sister So-and-So can come through that, I surely can.* God never fails us! He uses our trials for His glory and our good. We'll receive double for our trouble, just as our brother Job did. It's perfectly designed, if you ask me. I mean look at it — we'll never lose. That's why it's very important that we learn how to trust God fully with our lives. Don't think for one second that God wants us to go through trials just for the heck of it. He already has a plan of restoration for you; you need only allow Him to walk you through every dark place. That's why I honestly believe that Job had so much crazy faith in God. He knew God would bring him out, some way and somehow.

If we look very carefully at past events in our lives, we will see where God made ways out of no way for us ... whether we realized it or not. Some of us may claim we did it on our own, insist that a *human* someone came along and blessed us, or proclaim that "the paycheck came right on time." No, it was ALL GOD! I honestly believe God has everything to do with "all of a sudden" moments. If our breakthrough was something we caused to happen on our own, we could have already done so, correct? Exactly.

If you are going through, remember: It's up to you to stay focused on the Word of God and the things of God to emerge victorious. As your ultimate Source, He will provide you with everything you need. Begin to praise Him now.

You'll see, reading Job's story, that he had skeptical friends who believed he must have done something wrong to have brought on his misfortunes. You'll see evidence of Job's self-righteousness. You'll see how he questioned God (got pissed at God is more like it; who hasn't done that a time or two?) and how God got him straight. I *really* love how God got in Job's behind, corrected him, then gracefully blessed/restored him with even greater than he had before.

Job's story, which I'll take from the New Living Translation, starts here:

Job 1:1-3

There was once a man named Job who lived in the land of Uz. He was blameless — a man of complete integrity. He feared God and stayed away from evil. He had seven sons and three daughters. He owned 7,000 sheep, 3,000 camels, 500 teams of oxen, and 500 female donkeys. He also had many servants. He was, in fact, the richest person in that entire area.

Now this is when his testing began.

Job 1:6-12:

> One day the members of the heavenly court came to present themselves before the Lord, and the Accuser, Satan, came with them. "Where have you come from?" the Lord asked Satan. Satan answered the Lord, "I have been patrolling the earth, watching everything that's going on." Then the Lord asked Satan, "Have you noticed My servant Job? He is the finest man in all the earth. He is blameless — a man of complete integrity. He fears God and stays away from evil." Satan replied to the Lord, "Yes, but Job has good reason to fear God. You have always put a wall of protection around him and his home and his property. You have made him prosper in everything he does. Look how rich he is! But reach out and take away everything he has, and he will surely curse you to your face!" "All right, you may test him," the Lord said to Satan. "Do whatever you want with every-

thing he possesses, but don't harm him physically." So Satan left the Lord's presence.

What I really like about this story is that God had this much confidence in Job.

As the story goes, Job was visited by three messengers in a row who came to tell him that all his livestock had or been stolen or died via natural disaster and that all his servants had died or been killed. Then came a fourth messenger, who told him that his children had died, also via natural disaster. Job's reaction? After tearing his robe and shaving his head, he *fell down and worshipped God!* The takeaway: No matter what the enemy may throw our way, God's power, which resides in us, enables us to stand strong if we, like Job, stay faithful to Him. Even when we miss the mark and fall, we can get back up and try again because of the God we serve.

I love what God says to Satan in Job 2:3, when the members of the heavenly court presented themselves again before before Him and Satan reports that he's still been checking out things on earth.

> **Then the Lord asked Satan, "Have you noticed my servant Job? He is the finest man in all the earth. He is blameless — a man of complete integrity. He fears God and stays away from evil. And he has maintained his integrity, even though you urged me to harm him without cause."**

In Verses 4-6, Satan secures permission to make a second attempt to get Job to turn away from God:

> **Satan replied to the Lord, "Skin for skin! A man will give up everything he has to save his life. But reach out and take away his health, and he will surely curse you to your face!" "All right, do with him as you please," the Lord said to Satan. "But spare his life."**

God said, "Do with him as you please. But spare his life." That, to me, is absolute *love*. See, no matter what the enemy tries, he'll NEVER be able to take our lives unless we give up completely.

I also love how Job reacted to that attempt in verses 7-10:

> **So Satan left the Lord's presence and he struck Job with terrible boils from head to foot. Job scraped his skin with a piece of broken pottery as he sat among the ashes. His wife said to him, "Are you still trying to maintain your integrity? Curse God and die." But Job replied, "You talk like a foolish woman. Should we accept only good things from the hand of God and never anything bad?" So in all this, Job said nothing wrong.**

I can imagine God sitting there with so much confidence through Job's test, knowing what He had instilled in Job. He has equipped us all with what Job had. We just have to tap into it, knowing that God has our best interests at heart and that whatever our problem might be, it too shall pass.

Now don't get it twisted; Later during his ordeal, Job did curse the day he was born. Many of us do the very same thing without having endured nearly as much as our brother Job: "Why me? Why not them? They're doing much worse stuff then I'm doing — and they're getting away with it! I wish I'd never been born!" (Well, maybe that was just me acting that way.).

Can you relate to Job in Chapter 3:1-10?

> At last Job spoke, and he cursed the day of his birth. He said: "Let the day of my birth be erased, and the night I was conceived. Let that day be turned to darkness. Let it be lost even to God on high, and let no light shine on it. Let the darkness and utter gloom claim that day for its own. Let a black cloud overshadow it, and let the darkness terrify it. Let that night be blotted off the calendar, never again to be counted among the days of the year, never again to appear among the months. Let that night be childless. Let it have no joy. Let those who are experts at cursing — whose cursing could rouse Leviathan — curse that day. Let its morning stars remain dark. Let it hope for light, but in vain; may it never see the morning light. Curse that day for failing to shut my mother's womb, for letting me be born to see all this trouble."

I don't know about you, but my "bruh" was seriously going through it! He wanted his very existence to be wiped away. I've been in this place a couple times before. It's called being in a deep, dark depression, or being suicidal. I mean, I wanted God to take me right away, and I got very angry when He didn't. "Why do you have me here?" I asked Him. "Is it just to let others mistreat me constantly?" I was going through so much … back-to-back trials. It was very hard for me to comprehend that a loving God would allow me to go through this kind of torture and not do anything about it — well, at least when I wanted Him to. I later realized that the true beauty of God shows when He allows us to go through adversity, all the while keeping us and showing His love, grace and mercy. He's just awesome like that. He knows how things will end. He ensures that we'll come out better than we were when we entered our valley experience!

Trusting God is a must for real. Who else can bring you out stronger, wiser, more compassionate, after you go through storms that were meant to destroy you? Nobody but Him!

I know this much because for one, His Word tells me so, and two, my life experiences have shown me so. God has had to put me in my place a time or two, just as He did Job. I felt that some things I'd experienced, I shouldn't have had to go through. I'd be fussing, telling God about Himself, when my loving Father would remind me of Who He was to me and how He chose me, rather than my choosing Him.

I'm about to share some more Scriptures from Job's story. Chapter 7:1-16 is an illustration of how we today complain and make comparisons — as if that really moves God!

> "Is not all human life a struggle? Our lives are like that of a hired hand, like a worker who longs for the shade, like a servant waiting to be paid. I, too, have been assigned months of futility, long and weary nights of misery. Lying in bed, I think, 'When will it be morning?' But the night drags on, and I toss till dawn. My body is covered with maggots and scabs. My skin breaks open, oozing with pus. My days fly faster than weaver's shuttle. They end without hope. O God, remember that my life is but a breath, and I will never again feel happiness. You see me now, but not for long. You will look for me, but I will be gone. Just as a cloud dissipates and vanishes, those who die will not come back. They are gone forever from their home — never to be seen again. I cannot keep from speaking. I must express my anguish. My bitter soul must complain. Am I a sea monster or a dragon that you must place me under guard? I think, 'My bed will comfort me, and sleep will ease my misery,' but then you shatter me with dreams and terrify me with visions. I would rather be strangled — rather die than suffer like this. I hate my life and don't want to go on living. Oh, leave me alone for my few remaining days."

I don't know about you, but that has totally been me, once or twice! Sad, but so true. I just didn't want to be here enduring those painful, embarrassing situations. I also can understand how the enemy/innerme can convince people to commit suicide or at least fall into a deep depression and stay cooped up in the house, not wanting any human contact at all. But I also know a beautiful Man named Jesus, God's Son, Who died to save you. He will fight for you if you let Him. He can set you free from situations that have been holding you down. Just cry out to Him; I promise He will not let you down. If the situation seems to be lingering, know this much: He's working on your behalf behind the scenes. Just keep believing and trusting and praising His Holy Name, and He's sure to bring you out.

Further on in Job's story, you'll see that he insisted on his innocence and asked why the wicked weren't punished. He began to take on a self-righteous attitude and mess up in the sight of God. That's when God began to put him in his place! Mind you, this doesn't start until more than 30 chapters later. The Bible doesn't say exactly how long Job suffered, but we can safely say that his suffering lasted a while.

However long it took, breakthrough did come.

Job 38:1-11:

> **Then the Lord answered Job from the whirlwind: "Who is this that questions My wisdom with such ignorant words? Brace yourself like a man, because I have some questions for you, and you must answer**

them. Where were you when I laid the foundation of the earth? Tell me, if you know so much. Who determines its dimensions and stretched out the surveying line? What supports its foundations, and who laid its cornerstone as the morning stars sang together and all the angels shouted for joy? Who kept the sea inside its boundaries as it burst from the womb, and as I clothed it with clouds and wrapped it in thick darkness? For I locked it behind barred gates, limiting its shores. I said, 'This far and no farther will you come. Here your proud waves must stop!'"

God goes on to make His point in Job 38:19-21 …

"Where does light come from, and where does darkness go? Can you take each to its home? Do you know how to get there? But of course you know all this! For you were before it was all created, and you are so very experienced!"

and in Job 40:1-2 …

Then the Lord said to Job, "Do you still want to argue with the Almighty? You are God's critic, but do you have the answers?"

Finally, in verses 4-5, Job begins to gets a clue.

Then Job replied to the Lord, "I am nothing — how could I ever find the answers? I will cover my mouth with my hand. I have said too much already. I have nothing more to say."

We see in Chapter 42, verses 1-17, that Job did go on to say more ... but this time, he said all the right things!

> **Then Job replied to the Lord: "I know that you can do anything, and no one can stop you. You asked, 'Who is this that questions my wisdom with such ignorance?' It is I — and I was talking things I knew nothing about, things far too wonderful for me. You said, 'Listen and I will speak! I have some questions for you, and you must answer them.' I had only heard about you before, but now I have seen you with my own eyes.** (This is my favorite part. We all fall short in this area until we get to know God for ourselves and humbly repent. OK; back to the Scripture.) **I take back everything I said, and I sit in dust and ashes to show my repentance." After the Lord had finished speaking to Job, He said to Eliphaz the Temanite: "I am angry with you and your two friends, for you have not spoken accurately about me, as my servant Job has. So take seven bulls and seven rams and go to My servant Job and offer a burnt offering for yourselves. My servant Job will pray for you, and I will accept his prayer on your behalf. I will not treat you as you deserve, for you have not spoken accurately about me, as my servant Job has." So Eliphaz the Temanite, Bildad the Shuhite, and Zophar the Naamathite did as the Lord commanded them, and the Lord accepted Job's prayer. When Job prayed for his friends, the**

Lord restored his fortunes. In fact, the Lord gave him twice as much as before! Then all his brothers, sisters, and former friends came and feasted with him in his home. And they consoled him and comforted him because of all the trials the Lord had brought against him. And each of them brought him a gift of money and a gold ring. So the Lord blessed Job in the second half of his life even more than in the beginning. For now he had 14,000 sheep, 6,000 camels, 1,000 teams of oxen, and 1,000 female donkeys. He also gave Job seven more sons and three more daughters. He named his first daughter Jemimah, the second Keziah, and the third Keren-happuch. In all the land no women were as lovely as the daughters of Job. And their father put them into his will along with their brothers. Job lived 140 years after that, living to see four generations of his children and grandchildren. Then he died, an old man who had lived a long, full life.

I hope that Job's experiences will help you to see that you're not alone in the things you may go through, whether or not you brought them on yourself. I hope you'll see yourself, realize how easily we can fall into the same mental place Job did, remember how God had to get us in check, and see how He blesses us! Now don't act like *nothing* you've been through was your fault. Honestly, most of the messes we've been through, we've brought on ourselves. Yet, like Job, we also go through things because God said, "Have you considered my child _____?

If you are going through a trial that involves mistreatment by others, pray for them. Forgive them, for they know not what they do. Remember this: At some point, now or later, we will all need God's forgiveness, grace and mercy. Truth be told, many of us have prayers hindered and blessings held up due to unforgiveness of others and even of ourselves.

Repent and see how your life will begin to get better over time, even when you're going through your valley experiences. REMEMBER, TRUSTING GOD IS A MUST. EVEN WITH A MUSTARD SEED OF FAITH, JUST DO IT!

Here are two final Scriptures, also from the New Living Translation, that deal with trusting God. Use these during your prayer time.

Psalm 40:1-4:

> I waited patiently for the Lord to help me, and he turned to me and heard my cry. He lifted me out of the pit of despair, out of the mud and the mire. He set my feet on solid ground and steadied me as I walked along. He has given me a new song to sing, a hymn of praise to our God. Many will see what he has done and be amazed. They will put their trust in the Lord. Oh, the joys of those who trust in the

> Lord, who have no confidence in the proud or in those who worships idols.

Psalm 56:1-4:

> Oh God, have mercy on me, for people are hounding me. My foes attack me all day long. I am constantly hounded by those who slander me, and many are boldly attacking me. But when I am afraid, I will put my trust in you. I praise God for what he has promised. I trust in God, so why should I be afraid? What can mere mortals do to me?

I so pray that the wisdom God has given me to share in this book will bless you. I pray that after you read this, you will want to get to know the Savior in a deeper way. I pray this book causes you to rethink your walk with God to the point that real repentance, in whatever area of your life it's needed, will take place and you will begin to walk in the true freedom of Jesus Christ.

To the person reading this who has never tried Jesus: I pray that you will taste and see that He is truly awesome. No matter what has happened in your life, and no matter what you may think about Him, He loves you ... and He would love to have a chance to show you His love. I'm not talking about fake love — that conditional love we give one another. He desires to give you ALL OF HIM. Come on and try Him. What do you have to lose? If you *don't* try Him, you'll lose your soul! Please don't be so stubborn and cold-hearted that you refuse to give a chance to the One Who gave His life for you. Take it from me. I was someone who had nothing going good for herself, but He made sure I understood that He still had need of me. That's real love! Think of all the people who claimed they loved you, but left you when you didn't say or do what they wanted you to say or do.

I pray that the Holy Spirit brings about a conviction in you that results in real deliverance, healing, and restoration. In Second Corinthians 5:20-21, the Apostle Paul wrote that *"we are Christ's ambassadors; God is making his appeal through us. We speak for Christ when we plead, "Come back to God!" For God made Christ, who never sinned, to be the offering for our sin, so that we could be made right with God through Christ"* (NLT)

Become the new creature in Christ Jesus that you were designed to be. **DON'T LET THE ENEMY/INNERME KILL YOU OFF!**

In Jesus Christ's Name I pray for you, expecting great manifestation. Amen!

CHAPTER SIX

Let's Start Together

When I say, "Let's start together," I really mean that. I'm not one to put you out there to drown. I'm here to help you along on your journey.

Starting anything new — whether it's a new job, new school, new relationship or first-time parenthood — can be a little scary. But it can also be very exciting, right?

Unfortunately, some of us never get past Go. Scary beginnings can cause us to become mentally stuck ... and *stay* stuck. The years pass, and we think we're over the issue; we think we've matured. But in reality, we've just numbed the pain of whatever threw us off track in the first place. We'll never really learn how to live in the now, and enjoy our journey, until we hit rock bottom and come to ourselves, as the Prodigal Son did in the parable Jesus told in Luke 15. When we come to ourselves, we realize that only Jesus can help us. By now, low self-esteem, doubt, unforgiveness and other strongholds have set in ... all because we never took the time to move past that scary new beginning.

Our lack of confidence in ourselves starts, for the most part, in our youth, stemming from such things as high parental expectations, ridicule and rejection by peers, and a lack of self-acceptance. We wish we'd been born someone else, born into in a different family. I can speak for myself here. One thing you're learning about me as we walk this journey together is that I don't mind telling my truth. That's what's wrong with a lot of us. We don't like telling the naked truth about ourselves because we're afraid of what others may have to say. Truth be told, that's the only way to freedom. That's the very way to break the enemy's control of your mind and therefore your life.

One of the enemy's/innerme's tactics for keeping you bound is to keep you in fear of what others may say about you and your situation. (If I may be real with you, and I shall, the people you are so afraid of telling your business are battling issues also ... they need freedom from bondage themselves!) Falling prey to that fear, we remain so firmly stuck in our bad beginnings and our strongholds that when the Lord *does* give us a new start on life, we squander the opportunity ... or we run from it, saying, "This is too good to be true." Let me help you out right here. EVERYTHING the Lord God does is good and true. So, why do we run from what's good and true? Because we can't see who we really are or who we were created to be. At some point, we've got to learn that we are "fearfully and wonderfully made" (Psalm 139:14) by God for His purpose.

I understand; believe me, I do. Again, I've had a lot of not-so-good moments in my life, and I have reached the point of feeling that ending my life *had* to be the best option. I sure tried ... more than once, actually. Yet, God said "NO! Your soul belongs to me!" And I'm forever grateful. Thank You, Lord Jesus, for the grace and mercy that You bestowed upon me, as well as whoever is reading this. And to whoever is reading this, it's all right to give Him some praise. HALLELUJAH!!!

See, our lives don't belong to us. Some of us endured things that were downright awful, especially during our youth. Believe this much: God knows all about that and wants so badly to redeem the time for us. But we've got to let Him! We've got to let ALL of the baggage go. We've got to drop those bags off in the dumpster and leave them. Some things are not to be recycled. That's another way we get stuck in our beginnings ... recycling, or rethinking, hurtful experiences. We'll think, *I've got this. I'm OK. I'm grown/older now. I'm doing all right for myself.* I remember using the phrase, "I'm good." I still use it from time to time — until the Holy Spirit corrects me. "I'm good" is a lie we tell ourselves and our loved ones as a way to cover up our fear or our denial — "I can take care of myself." Even those of us who have college degrees, money, fancy houses and cars are telling ourselves that same lie: "I'm good." We don't see the enemy sitting back laughing and planning our downfall.

If this is you, it doesn't have to be this way. God still has need of you. He really loves you. Stop trying to understand *how*, and just know that he does. Believe and receive it by faith. Yes, despite all the things that have happened in your life, He still loves you. You may be asking yourself, *If He loves me, why didn't He stop my cousin from touching me inappropriately? Why didn't He stop my father from beating me while he was drunk and high? Why didn't He stop me from being bullied by my peers and becoming a hateful overachiever as a result? Why did He allow my loved one to die, after we prayed for a healing? Why did He allow my friend and my loved one to be murdered? Why did He allow those miscarriages? Why did He allow my children to be taken from me and leave me unable to have any more?* I've had a few questions myself.

Guess what? God has heard them all. Maybe you'll get answers to your questions; maybe not. Just know this: None of the things that happened to you was caused by God. Blame it on the enemy — and the sinful nature of the people involved. Sin entered and caused death to creep into our lives.

Why did God let those hateful, hurtful things happen? Let's go back to the beginning of time. When God created the earth, darkness existed. Yet, God saw that it was good to have light. God prevailed over the prince of power of the air ... Satan. So, the enemy had to creep in some kind of way. He crept in the same way he often does ... by causing God's creation to become disobedient. It was disobedience that brought about our sinful nature. The enemy has no power, except for the power people give him as a result of his deception and persuasion tactics.

Think about this for a moment: Everything God created was good, as is pointed out in Chapter 1 of the book of Genesis ... the book that tells of mankind's spiritual fall through Adam and Eve's disobedience. Some might ask, "Why did He put the tree of the knowledge of good and evil in the Garden of Eden if He knew that Adam and Eve would eat from it and become separated from Him?" Remember this: God gave man free will. We're all free to make our own choices. God didn't create us to be puppets. Yet, He knew we would need His guidance, just as young children need the guidance of their parents. Children don't always obey, correct? It was the same with Adam and Eve. They had to learn the hard way, as most of us do. Why? Well, one might say it's because we're curious creatures. Even when we know right from wrong, we sometimes choose to do wrong. Sin entered Eden when Eve, then Adam, gave in to the serpent's temptation and chose to disobey instructions by eating the fruit from the tree. The enemy can only present something to people and play mind games with us. It's up to us to decide whether we will entertain his thoughts or obey wisdom as she speaks.

Everything has a place and a part to play in life. God is order. God is good. The enemy is evil. He is the father of sin, and sin leads to death. His attempts to destroy us start mainly with mind games. If you entertain the wrong thoughts, you'll eventually begin to do wrong. I know this all too well. Yet, I've also had the pleasure of pondering the things that are true, and honest, and just, and pure, and lovely, and of good report (Philippians 4:8).

We have the advantage of being able to defeat our past hurts and failures simply by giving up our sinful ways of thinking and retraining our hearts according to God's original plan. If you die to self, begin to trust God and truly surrender, what a beautiful life you will have! This comes from someone who was broken, who was full of self-hatred and unforgiveness, but who also had a thirst for real love and affection. I had to surrender to my perfect, all-knowing, loving God before I could begin to love my imperfect self. Then and only then did I begin to understand what I do about the Holy Trio — God the Father, God the Son, and God the Holy Spirit — and Their love for us.

I challenge you to start your day off by giving God free range with all of you. You'll begin to see daily change. Now don't get me wrong; some days you won't always like the truths God shows you, or the hidden scars He reveals. But I promise, it's all for your good and God's glory!

The Word tells us, via Romans 8:28, that *"all things work together for good to them that love God, to them who are the called according to his purpose"* (KJV). This is the best way I can explain to you about trusting God in all things, and with all things, that matter to you. You've got to start someday; why not now? Remember, **DON'T LET THE ENEMY/ INNERME KILL YOU OFF!**

CHAPTER SEVEN

How Do You Trust God?

*A*fter all I've mentioned previously about trust, you would think that was that. But I beg to differ. When I hear the word "how," I often think I'm back in English class. When "how" starts a sentence, I often think of *showing* something: "How do you … "? There needs to be a demonstration, which signifies action.

So, let me start showing you some ways to trust God … ways that were taught me by the Holy Spirit and at times, my spiritual mentor, Delois Riley.

When I finally got serious about my life and about doing God's will, I would begin my day with the Lord's prayer as revealed in Matthew 6:9-13, KJV: *"Our Father which art in heaven, Hallowed be thy name. Thy kingdom come, Thy will be done in earth, as it is in heaven. Give us this day our daily bread. And forgive us our debts, as we forgive our debtors. And lead us not into temptation, but deliver us from evil: For thine is the kingdom, and the power, and the glory, for ever. Amen."* It also states in Matthew 6:8 that God already knows what you have need of before you even ask. I hear your question: "Well, why do I need to ask, if He already knows?"

It's called faith. It takes faith to walk with God and advance His kingdom. You've got to believe that He can and will make a way out of no way; that He will deliver, heal, and set free. The Word also says that without faith, it's impossible to please God (Hebrews 11:6).

All that I am today comes from my wholehearted trust in the God who made me and molded me for His purpose. Now don't get it twisted; I didn't get here overnight. It took some soul searching and denying my flesh all the worldly things I used to do and say. As I stated before, I had to get serious about my life as well as my children. I had a great desire to be so much more than what I was at that time in my life. Now I realize that God had that desire too, based on what He told the prophet Jeremiah: *"For I know the thoughts that I think toward you ... thoughts of peace, and not of evil, to give you an expected end"* (Jeremiah 29:11, KJV).

You know what? The Word of God is all we really need. If you take the time to read it, God's Word by itself will teach you, step by step, how to trust Him. It takes a committed mind to learn, however. You've got to *"study to shew thyself approved unto God, a workman that needeth not to be ashamed, rightly dividing the word of truth"* (2 Timothy 2:15, KJV) and hide the Word in your heart (Psalm 119:11). I look at it like this: Just as you invest time and energy into getting to know someone with whom you're interested in having an earthly relationship, you need to invest time and energy into studying the Word in order to have a relationship with God and get what you need from Him. That's how I have gotten to know God and trust Him ... reading and studying His Word.

One thing I've come to find out is that our Father God already knows that it may be a process for us to get to where we put all our trust in Him. I had to learn the hard way. I know that not all of us have experienced back-to-back hardships, but I've noticed that some have managed to avoid quite a few mistakes simply by applying and obeying God's word by faith. That wasn't me at first. I was one of those "I have to see it for myself" kind of followers.

You may be saying, "I've spent time in God's face and in His Word, but I'm *still* experiencing nonstop tribulation." If that's your story, maybe you need to check your heart and your motives. My word tells me, *"If ye be willing and obedient, ye shall eat the good of the land"* (Isaiah 1:19). Psalm 84:11 states that *"no good thing will he withhold from them that walk uprightly."* And I love what Verse 12 says that *"blessed is the man that trusteth in thee* [God]" (all KJV).

What I've noticed in 11 years of being truly sold out to Christ Jesus is that we, as followers, are quick to *say* that we trust Him. But do we really? In all too many cases, when we feel our prayers have gone unanswered or have not been answered in the way we desire, we start to fall apart. We begin to play the blame game: "She's the reason," "He's the reason," "Maybe I'm just not good enough for God to answer my prayers." Then, along with doubt, depression begins to arise. These are lies and tricks of the enemy. We must remember that it's the enemy's job to steal, kill, and destroy (John 10:10).

I come back to the issue of conditional trust, which can leave room for the enemy to do what he does to us. Just as we make the mistake of loving others conditionally, we trust God 'n' them conditionally! Yes, I said, "'n' them," including God's other Persons: Jesus and the Holy Spirit. We say we love the Lord. Yet when things don't fall into place the way *we* want it to, or God allows us to go through an experience that will bring about correction to better us, we just *stop*. We stop singing praises unto our all-knowing, perfect, loving Holy Trio. Praising God only when things are going well means we're allowing the enemy to steal our peace, our joy … and our love. And let's not forget: These were given freely to us by the One and Only Christ Jesus.

Think about it like this: We are still spiritually immature if we can so easily fall prey to the enemy's mind games and revert to this kind of behavior. Let's always remember to ask God for His wisdom, His knowledge and His understanding concerning any matter in our lives so that we may be able to grow spiritually and mature in all things concerning God and His kingdom.

Search out His Word. That's how you'll know God's heartbeat and that's how you can begin the journey of trusting Him. **DON'T LET THE ENEMY/INNERME KILL YOU OFF!**

Prayers to build your trust in God

Dear Father,

Thank You for this beautiful day. Thank You for life. Thank You for Your unconditional love for me and my family. Thank You for healing us — not just in a physical sense, but also healing our minds, because that's where the battles begin. We need all the healing we can get. We need to be made whole by You, Father God.

Thank You for making us strong in the power of Your might, Lord. Thank You for the favor that You have placed our lives. Keep us, Holy Spirit. Help us along our journeys. Help us daily as we walk with the crosses we've taken up, striving to be like the Lord Jesus.

Thank You for peace, love, and joy in You, Christ Jesus. Have Your way. Help us to allow You to do You! In Christ Jesus' Name I pray these things. AMEN!

Dear Father,

I'm humbled unto You. Keep having Your way in my life. I want to follow You more now than ever. Thank You for giving me the desires of my heart.

Thank You, Big Brother Jesus, for interceding daily for me, especially in my broken places. You remind me that You're always there, even when I'm too scared or too stubborn to realize it. You are ALWAYS here with me.

Holy Spirit, thank You for teaching me how to pray and what to pray for. I don't want fleshly desires anymore; I want what God wants me to have. Help me daily, Holy Spirit, to follow Your lead. I want to learn all the more how to not be moved off my rock and my foundation — Christ Jesus — and how not to be moved by any uncomfortable or unpleasant situation that may come my way. It is my desire to help others overcome, in and through the power of Jesus.

It is in Jesus' Name that I pray this prayer, Father God. Thank You for listening and answering! AMEN.

Dear Father,

I just want to thank You for giving me life. Thank You for giving me another chance to get things right with You. Thank You for the newness; thank You for ordering my steps in You. I'm learning how to allow You to take full control of my life and everything that concerns me. Help me to renew my mind instead of falling back on the things I've been taught about You from a "religiosity" standpoint. I give Your Holy Spirit free reign to teach me all the things I need to know about You. I want to have a relationship with You like no other! I've had failed relationships with family, significant others and friends, and I am so ready for change. I'm ready to experience the very things that those rooted and grounded in You rave about. I'm ready to taste and see how good You really are.

Thank You for listening to and answering my prayer. In Christ Jesus' Name I pray, AMEN!

Dear Father,

Thank You for showing me how to love myself; to see myself as You see me. I'm learning that in order to trust You, I want and need to know how You see me. I have allowed society, family and friends to shape who I am today instead of flowing in what You created me to be. I don't know my real identity. Create in me a clean heart, Father God, and renew Your spirit within me. I know there's more to me than that which is defined by the life I'm currently living. I want all that You have for me and my family. Your Word says that You have great plans for me. I know that it won't be easy, but I'm ready to walk it out, trusting You with all my heart, my mind, and my soul. In Christ Jesus' name I pray this prayer unto You, Father God. AMEN.

These are prayers I found myself writing to the Father in my daily journal. They got me through some scary and lonely times. I will share more of these prayers in the following chapters. I hope they will help you along the way as well.

CHAPTER EIGHT

"How Can I Mature Spiritually?"

*I*f you're a baby Christian — or a Christian who finds himself or herself spiritually stuck, going around the same mistake mountain — this question may be on your heart: "How can I mature spiritually?"

I'm glad you asked!

First things first: Stop letting every setback kill you off. Stop letting every "not now" answer to your prayers for breakthrough and deliverance kill you off! The experiences God allows you to go through are experiences He uses for your good, as indicated in 1 Peter 5:10: *"But the God of all grace, who hath called us unto his eternal glory by Christ Jesus, after that ye have suffered a while, make you perfect, stablish, strengthen, settle you"* (KJV)

To get where God is wanting us to go, we're going to have to endure some things. Some of us will endure more than others; yet, we all are going to mature in our promised trials and tribulations. This is pointed out in Romans 5:3 — *"And not only so, but we glory in tribulations also: knowing that tribulation worketh patience"* (also KJV) — as well as James 1:2-8:

> **My brethren, count it all joy when ye fall into divers temptations; Knowing this, that the trying of your faith worketh patience. But let patience have her perfect work, that ye may be perfect and entire, wanting nothing. If any of you lack wisdom, let him ask of God, that giveth to all men liberally, and upbraideth not; and it shall be given him. But let him ask in faith, nothing wavering. For he that wavereth is like a wave of the sea driven with the wind and tossed. For let not that man think that he shall receive anything of the Lord. A double minded ma is unstable in all his ways.**

One thing I've noticed when a person lacks spiritual maturity is that he or she always wants to give up at the first sign of trouble. We need to remember what Jesus said in Matthew 24 when He talked about the coming days and the persecution of the faithful: The one who endures to the end will be saved (Verse 13). That's how you'll win. Learn how to endure in the developing stages of your faith. And when things begin to get a little hard to handle, and believe me they will, you'll have a foundation – Jesus — to fall back on.

Now, don't get me wrong. I'm not telling anyone to be ignorant and stay in an abusive relationship of any kind, whether it be physical, mental or emotional. Nor am I telling anyone to allow their God-given spiritual gifts to be pimped, especially in this day and time. Please make sure that you put on your full armor of God daily so that you won't be easily fooled or worse, find yourself trapped in some sort of religious cult. (I've noticed these things happenings to babes in Christ Jesus!) Ask God to lead and guide you daily by His Holy Spirit, trust Him, and obey Him. Yes, you'll miss the mark sometimes. The key is not to wallow in your failure. Get back up, repent, and continue your walk with Him. You'll begin to understand and appreciate this as you mature in the things of God. Ask Him for wisdom, knowledge, understanding and strength to endure trials and tribulations. Do this and you'll be able to stand against all the plot and plans of the enemy/innerme to destroy you!

Another way to grow spiritually and survive the attacks of the enemy/innerme: Stop allowing yourself to become easily offended and learn how to forgive quickly. Remind yourself that forgiveness is for your own spiritual growth as well as your mental, emotional and physical health. Colossians 3:13 tells of how we, having "put off the old man" and "put on the new man," are to conduct ourselves and treat each other: *"Forbearing one another, and forgiving one another, if any man have a quarrel against any: even as Christ forgave you, so also do ye"* (KJV). Study this verse as you delve deeper into the Word of God and allow the Holy Spirit to give you insight into the Lord Jesus Christ.

Do not assume that just because you've been in church your whole life, you know everything there is to know about the Bible or about God. Remember, there's *always* something new that we can learn daily, even from Scriptures with which we think we're familiar. Don't be one of those individuals who can't be corrected, told something new, or told something again. If God is telling us the same thing He told us before, but through a different source, that means we disregarded it the first time, or didn't handle it the way God intended for us to handle it. Beloved, it's time to WAKE UP! Stop being easily offended. Forgive quickly. With spiritual maturity, gained through the Holy Spirit, comes the realization that we need to get a new revelation from God daily. Yes! He speaks daily. But we're not always listening. The Bible has the answers; I guarantee it. Consider these Scriptures:

> **Grace and peace be multiplied unto you through the knowledge of God, and of Jesus our Lord, According as his divine power hath given unto us all things that pertain unto life and godliness, through the knowledge of him that hath called us to glory and virtue: Whereby are given unto us exceeding great and precious promises: that by these ye might be partakers of the divine nature, having escaped the corruption that is in the world through lust. And beside this, giving all diligence, add to your faith virtue; and to virtue knowledge; And to knowledge temperance;**

and to temperance patience; and to patience godliness; And to godliness brotherly kindness; and to brotherly kindness charity. For if these things be in you, and abound, they make you that ye shall neither be barren nor unfruitful in the knowledge of our Lord Jesus Christ. But he that lacketh these things is blind, and cannot see afar off, and hath forgotten that he was purged from his old sins. Wherefore the rather, brethren, give diligence to make your calling and election sure: for if ye do these things, he shall never fall: For so an entrance shall be ministered unto you abundantly into the everlasting kingdom of our Lord and Savior Jesus Christ. (2 Peter 1:2-11, KJV)

Wherefore I also, after I heard of your faith in the Lord Jesus, and love unto all the saints, Cease not to give thanks for you, making mention of you in my prayers; that the God of our Lord Jesus Christ, the Father of glory, may give unto you the spirit of wisdom and revelation in the knowledge of him: (Ephesians 1:15-17, KJV)

Oh, I dare not close out this chapter without saying one more very important thing about how we can spiritually mature concerning the things of God: QUIT BLAMING EVERYBODY ELSE for the choices you made that have you in the situation you're in. Yes, many of us have been wronged. Some of us have had unhuman, unspeakable things done to us. But how we act in return determines our outcome. God will deal with the offender according to His timing. No one on this earth can sow any good or bad seeds without reaping the appropriate harvest (Galatians 6:7). So, stop trying to be God and taking matters into your own hands. It will only make things worse for you, not the offender. When you begin to allow God to change your mind, heart and emotions in any adverse situation, that's when you know that you are spiritually maturing in the things of God.

By the way, you must also *ask forgiveness of anyone you have wronged* as well as asking God's forgiveness for wronging that person. Don't get all self-righteous and consider yourself to be so good that you have never hurt someone! Just sit still in God's presence and ask Him to show you any instances in which you mistreated someone and didn't repent for it. Believe me, He will show you! I thought I'd never wronged anyone … until I sat myself down at the feet of Jesus in pure worship and He so tenderly showed D'Antquonese her true self. That was one of the best experiences I've had with the Lord God. I was shown how to be real with myself. And He allowed me to repair some relationships with people I had offended.

Pray for your enemies and remember to pray for yourself. **DON'T LET THE ENEMY/INNERME KILL YOU OFF!**

Prayers for spiritual maturity

Dear Father,

I'm so thankful for the newness of this journey on which You have me. I haven't been Your best-behaved child, but You already knew that. Thank You for showing me how to love myself and showing me that You love me all the more. Thank You for all the blessings You have bestowed upon me today. Thank You for changing my way of thinking, especially when I get emotional and believe I have every right to do so. You are always teaching me about self-control and how to apply it in my most emotional moments. I'm so very grateful to You, my Heavenly Trio.

In Jesus Christ's mighty Name, I pray this prayer. Father God, thank You for listening. AMEN!

Dear Father,

Thank You for seeing fit to bless me with Your grace and mercy today. Today, I choose to allow myself to forgive those who have wronged me in any way. I also ask You, Father God, to forgive me of my wrongs — those that I know of and those that I am unaware of or have forgotten. I also pray for those I have wronged. I pray that You bless each of them with a healed heart, mind, and soul. Thank You, Father God, for giving me the mindset to pray in this manner. Thank You for blessing my mind and heart. I grow more in love with You daily.

It is in Jesus Christ's mighty Name that I pray these things, Father God. Thank You for listening. AMEN!

Dear Father,

Thank You for life today. Thank You for being my very present help in times of trouble. Thank You for keeping me near the cross today, especially when the enemy brought the spirit of frustration my way. I know there are some things I could have done differently and handled better. Help me, Holy Spirit, to keep my tone of voice kind and gentle when I'm expressing my feelings and opinions to others. Keep me from come off as too strong or obnoxious when I mean no harm. I thank You, Lord. In Jesus Christ's mighty Name, AMEN.

Dear Father,

Thank You so much for this beautiful day. Regardless of how it has started out, I will bless Your Holy name. My situation will not lessen my praise of You. You deserve all my praise. Thank You for keeping me, even in those moments during which I couldn't care less whether You kept me or not. Thank You for seeing past the petty, bratty attitudes I have at times. Thank You for giving me the mindset to praise You anyhow.

Thank You for teaching us how to be both Kingdom-minded and earthly good, so that You may get Your glory from our lives and that all things work out for our good. Thank You for Your Word, which prophesied to our dry bones so that they might live. In Jesus Christ's mighty Name, I believe and receive what I've prayed. AMEN!

CHAPTER NINE

Learning His Perfect Will for Your Life

"But seek ye first the kingdom of God, and his righteousness, and all these things shall be added unto you." — Matthew 6:33, KJV

This Scripture is highlighted in Chapter Three as my favorite. I know you're probably wondering why I didn't start the book with it, especially those of you who are Bible scholars. When was the last time you saw someone do what was best for them first? Exactly! If we did that, it would be awesome. Unfortunately, in most cases, we have to try things *our* way first, second, and third. It's not until we've almost allowed the enemy/innerme to kill us off that we finally say, "OK, Lord! What do You want from me?" That's certainly happened in my case.

Those of us who have been chosen to do great exploits for the Lord God normally go through hell and high water before we surrender to Him. Why? I don't know — it's just something we *do*. We do everything that we feel we're big and bad enough to do on our own. The inevitable result: We go through unnecessary mess. Yet, this mess proves to ultimately be what God uses to further His Kingdom. He always has a way to get His glory from our mistakes.

Truth be told, some of these experiences aren't mistakes. Some things we do out of self-sabotage or spite, but God overlooks our silly selves. (Lord, I just feel the need to thank You right here. I know I've done some things that were not only less than ideal, but downright mean. Hallelujah to the Lamb of God for dying on the cross for messed-up souls like mine! I truly want to say Thank You! See, sometimes you just need to take a praise break and give God what's due Him. If you begin to think about all the crazy things you have said or done in your life — knowing you don't deserve the grace and mercy so freely given you — you'll stop reading right now and give some "crazy praise" yourself!)

Now, back to my point. We often suffer through our negative situations forever and a day before we even *begin to think* about surrendering to God. Much of our tribulation doesn't have anything to do with God's *perfect* will, but rather His *permissive* will.

According to a Bible.org essay that answers the question: "Can you help me understand God's perfect will versus His permissive will?", God's perfect will is found in Romans 12:2: *"Don't copy the behavior and customs of this world, but let God transform you into a new person by changing the way you think [the renewing of your mind]. Then you will learn to know God's will for you, which is good and pleasing and perfect"* (NLT).

"Notice that here, turning one's back on the world, and having one's mind renewed (by God) enables [you] to discern and experience God's will for you, a will ... which is good, which is a delight to us and to God, and which has no flaws, no missing pieces — complete," writes the author of that essay.

God's permissive will comes out of His having given man free will. He allows us to make our own choices, even if they are sinful choices. "God allows man to reject the gospel, to willfully disobey His laws, to persecute the righteous, and so on," the writer at Bible.org continues. "But in all of this, God is still in control, and His purposes are being accomplished."

I personally believe that God allows us to go through all sorts of messed-up situations because He knows we'll eventually realize we can't make it without His help, and we'll surrender ourselves to His perfect will. Everything that has taken place, He will use for His glory and our good, as stated in Romans 8:28. Now I'm not saying for us to be out here all willy-nilly, doing any and everything on purpose and thinking that God's going to let that fly. Umm, sorry ... that's a lie you just told yourself. As Jesus reminded the devil in Matthew 4:7 during His testing time in the wilderness — "Thou shalt not tempt the Lord thy God." And please be *very* mindful that whatsoever you sow, that you will reap. But because of the grace and mercy we receive through the sacrifice of our Lord and Savior Jesus Christ, we don't reap the way we should! Hebrews 10:26-31 points out the fate of those who reject Jesus and continue on their sinful paths, after being told of Him:

> **Dear friends, if we deliberately continue sinning after we have received knowledge of the truth, there is no longer any sacrifice that will cover these sins. There is only the terrible expectation of God's judgment and the raging fire that will consume his enemies. For anyone who refused to obey the law of Moses was put to death without mercy on the testimony of two or three witnesses. Just think how much worse the punishment will be for those who have trampled on the Son of God, and have treated the blood of the covenant, which made us holy, as if it were common and unholy, and have insulted and disdained the Holy Spirit who brings God's mercy to us. For we know the one who said, "I will take revenge, I will pay them back." He also said, "The Lord will judge his own people." It is a terrible thing to fall into the hands of the living God. (NLT)**

Where do we find the first revelation of God's perfect will for man? Take a look at the first three chapters of Genesis (all reference NLT).

In Gen. 1:26-28, we find the first reference to God's creation of man.

> Then God said, "Let us make human beings in our own image, to be like us. They will reign over the fish in the sea, the birds in the sky, the livestock, all the wild animals on the earth, and the small animals that scurry along the ground." So God created human beings in his own image. In the image of God he created them; male and female he created them. Then God blessed them and said, "Be fruitful and multiply. Fill the earth and govern it. Reign over the fish in the sea, the birds in the sky, and all the animals that scurry along the ground."

Now, I want you to look at Genesis 2. We can't even begin to imagine how profound, majestic and perfect God's will for us was:

> This is the account of the creation of the heavens and the earth. When the Lord God made the earth and the heavens, neither wild plants nor grains were growing on the earth. For the Lord God had not yet sent rain to water the earth, and there were no people to cultivate the soil. Instead, springs came up from the ground and watered all the land. (**Gen. 2:4-6**)

Now I don't know about you, but that's awesome to me, especially considering that this is *not* how things are today. God's *perfect* will for His children gave way to His *permissive* will after the disobedience of His first two children. I again cite John 15:16, where Jesus tells His followers, "You didn't choose me, but I chose you." That's Word with which we can fight the enemy when he tries to make us feel worthless! God chose to keep us close to His heart, adopt us into His family through His Son, Christ Jesus, and enable us by His Holy Spirit.

Now, Verse 7 of Genesis 2 is where we get to the part about God's perfect will concerning male and female:

Then the Lord God formed the man from the dust of the ground. He breathed the breath of life into the man's nostrils, and the man became a living person.

Right here is another praise break for me because this thing just got real! Without God we're nothing. Without His Word of life, correction, and direction, we're lost. In the New Testament book of Jude, it's pointed out that we are spiritually dead, yet we're walking around here like we're OK and "we got this." Yet, we're spiritually dead to the things of God. We're lost when it comes to how to enjoy the biggest blessing of all — LIFE (Living Internally, For Eternity). We need the breath of God. We need His Son, Christ Jesus, to experience heaven on earth and live in eternity with the Godhead after our shells return to the dust. An eternal place is already prepared for those who accept Christ Jesus as their Lord and Savior.

A little further down in Genesis 2, God begins to reveal more of His perfect will for the man He created, who was called Adam.

1. God set Adam up in his own land, (Verse 8), made especially for him, and gave him dominion, or charge over all. Look at that! Adam was given a place of his own ... acres of real estate that he'd neither built nor toiled for. According to the perfect will of God, we who are believers are set apart from others so that God's glory may be revealed to those who do not believe on Him.

2. God had man's meals already planned. He was then given all seed-bearing plants – along with "beautiful" trees that produced "delicious" fruit (Gen. 1:29, 2:9). Look at how our eating habits have changed.

3. As a part of His perfect will, God gave us free will. But with that gift came a warning in Verses 15-17:

> **The Lord God placed the man in the Garden of Eden to tend and watch over it. But the Lord God warned him, "You may freely eat the fruit of every tree in the garden — except the tree of the knowledge of good and evil. If you eat its fruit, you are sure to die."**

4. God didn't want man to be alone; He saw that it wasn't good for him. He stated, "I will make a helper who is just right for him" (Verse 18). He saw that two were better than

one. That right there speaks volumes to my soul. God saw fit to make sure that we as humans had the *natural* help we needed, as well as the *spiritual* help that we get from Him.

5. Last yet not least: God made a woman, later called Eve, for Adam. In Verses 19-20, God formed all the wild animals and birds, and brought them to Adam to name, but there was still no helper just right for Adam.

> **So the Lord God caused the man to fall into deep sleep. While the man slept, the Lord God took out one of the man's ribs and closed up the opening. Then the Lord God made a woman from the rib, and he brought her to the man. "At last!" the man exclaimed. "This one is bone from my bone, and flesh from my flesh! She will be called 'woman,' because she was taken from 'man.'" This explains why a man leaves his father and mother and is joined to his wife, and the two are united into one. Now the man and his wife were both naked, but they felt no shame. (Verses 21-25)**

Now God's permissive comes into play after the disobedience of His children in the third chapter of Genesis, when the serpent shows up on the scene with his deception and lies. Remember earlier on, when God gave Adam instructions concerning the trees of the knowledge of good and evil — just like nowadays when God warns us not to do something because He already knows the consequences we will suffer? Yet, what do we often do? We listen to the enemy/innerme when he tells us that we surely won't die if we do this thing!

In Gen. 3:1-7, we see paradise lost:

> The serpent was the shrewdest of all the wild animals the Lord God had made. One day he asked the woman, "Did God really say you must not eat the fruit from any of the trees in the garden?" "Of course we may eat fruit from the trees in the garden," the woman replied. "It's only the fruit from the tree in the middle of the garden that we are not allowed to eat. God said, 'You must not eat it or even touch it; if you do, you will die." "You won't die!" the serpent replied to the woman. "God knows that your eyes will be opened as soon as you eat it, and you will be like God, knowing both good and evil." The woman was convinced. She saw that the tree was beautiful and its fruit looked delicious, and she wanted the wisdom it would give her. So she took some of the fruit and ate it. Then she gave some to her husband, who was with her, and he ate it, too. At that moment their eyes were opened, and they suddenly felt shame at their nakedness. So they sewed fig leaves together to cover themselves.

I've often wondered why we sometimes disregard God's warnings, especially when we know better. Well, the answer is here in the Scriptures, plain as day. Deception and lies began in the beginning! There's nothing new under the sun, as King Solomon pointed out in the book of Ecclesiastes.

Adam's and Eve's disobedience caused a great shift in God's perfect will for humanity. At first, everything was, as the Word puts it, good. But man's direct, daily contact with God, his ability to commune with God on a one-on-one level, is now put to an end. The Word shows, via Gen. 3:14-19, exactly where the permissive will of God begins:

> **Then God said to the serpent, "Because you have done this, you are cursed more than all animals, domestic and wild. You will crawl on your belly, groveling in the dust as long as you live. And I will cause hostility between you and the woman, and between your offspring and her offspring. He will strike your head, and you will strike his heel." Then He said to the woman, "I will sharpen the pain of your pregnancy, and in pain you will give birth. And you will desire to control your husband, but he will rule over you." And to the man he said, "Since you listened to your wife and ate from the tree whose fruit I commanded you not to eat, the ground is cursed because of you. It will grow thorns and thistles for you, though you will eat of its grains. By the sweat of your brow will you have food to eat until you return to the ground from which you were made. For**

you were made from the dust, and to the dust you will return."

Now I don't know about you all, but I see so many clear messages through these Scriptures alone! Because of them, I'm paying closer attention to certain things in my life. Yes, we are redeemed from bondage by the blood of Jesus, Who died to reconcile us to God and restored what we lost spiritually through Adam's fall: *"For Christ has already accomplished the purpose for which the law as given. As a result, all who believe in him are made right with God"* (Romans 10:4, NLT). The Word also says that who the Son (Jesus) has set free, is free indeed (John 8:36).

That is spiritual freedom. However, in the natural we still have to live by certain conditions. Women, we still suffer excruciating pain during childbirth ... some more than others. And men — along with women these days! — must still work for a living, eating by the sweat of their brow.

But before anyone gets it twisted when it comes to Gen. 3:17-19 and tries to say that men should not listen to their wives, let's make sure we clearly understand what God said here. When we speak with the voice of wisdom to our husbands, they can listen. Yet, that man still must obey the voice of God. If your husband does not know the voice of God as well as you do, that's where prayer and fasting comes in. Help him to get to that place in God, because you definitely want order in your house. You don't have to drive it down your husband's throat that he needs to get in position to hear from God; God says that *"with lovingkindness have I drawn thee"* (Jeremiah 31:3). Use the wisdom of God, especially when it comes to approaching your husband. This will make a world of difference in whether, and when, he realizes the importance of hearing from God concerning himself, you, and your family. And you you'll be able to walk in the *perfect* will of God, not His *permissive* will.

There's another example of God's perfect and permissive will that I would like to share with you. It concerns Abram (later Abraham) and Sarai (later Sarah) and it, too, comes from the book of Genesis ... Chapters 15-21, NLT. I will give you some examples from the New Testament as well. After this, you should have a clear understanding of what I mean by learning God's perfect will for your own life.

> **Some time later, the Lord spoke to Abram in a vision and said to him, "Do not be afraid, Abram, for I will protect you, and your reward will be great." But Abram replied, "O Sovereign Lord, what good are all your blessings when I don't even have a son? Since you've given me no children, Eliezer of Damascus, a servant in my household, will inherit all my wealth. You have given me no descendants of my own, so one of my servants will be my heir." Then the Lord said to him, "No, your servant will not be your heir, for you will have a son of your own who will be your heir." Then the Lord took Abram outside and said**

to him, "Look up into the sky and count the stars if you can. That's how many descendants you will have!" And Abram believed the Lord, and the Lord counted him as righteous because of his faith. (Gen. 15:1-6)

As you read about God's perfect will for Abram, I know you should be able to relate to how Abram responds to God — I know I can! God started off by approaching Abram in a vision. The first thing he said was, "Do not be afraid." Normally, our first reaction is fear when something new comes about in our lives. Why? Because it's new — and sometimes "new" doesn't always go the way we want or hope, even if it's a word given us by a prophet of God. (Even when we're dealing with prophecies, we have to remember that we only prophesy in part, according to 1 Cor. 13:9. God provides the "whole picture.")

I really love how transparent Abram was with God in his response to God's approach. I can relate to that also, because I'm very open and honest with God myself. I can be as wrong as two left feet, yet God will allow me to say whatever is on my heart. Then, He says to me, "Don't be afraid; I'm God. I've got you." See, God wants us to be real and honest with Him. He also wants us to trust Him and His plans for our lives. But like Abram, we argue with (and sometimes fight) God before we fully surrender to His perfect will.

Nonetheless, God not only promised to bless Abram with a son, He told Abram that he'd have as many descendants as the stars as he could see! Then God called Abram righteous, just because Abram believed Him. *Abram's faith in God's words* made him righteous. Not some act or deed. Just his faith. How mind-blowing is that? It's pretty doggone awesome to me. All I have to do is have faith in God — and that will please Him!

Now I'm going to skip over to Genesis 16 and share more of the story of Abram and Sarai and how God allowed His permissive will to take place in their lives due to lack of faith and impatience:

> **Now Sarai, Abram's wife, had not been able to bear children for him. But she had an Egyptian servant named Hagar. So Sarai said to Abram, "The Lord has prevented me from having children. Go and sleep with my servant. Perhaps I can have children through her." And Abram agreed with Sarai's proposal. So Sarai, Abram wife, took Hagar the Egyptian servant and gave her to Abram as a wife. (This happened ten years after Abram had settled in the land of Canaan.) So Abram had sexual relations with Hagar, and she became pregnant. But when Hagar knew she was pregnant, she began to treat her mistress, Sarai, with contempt. Then Sarai said to Abram, "This is all your fault! I put my servant into your arms, but now that she's pregnant she**

treats me with contempt. The Lord will show who's wrong — you or me!" Abram replied, "Look, she is your servant, so deal with her as you see fit." Then Sarai treated Hagar so harshly that she finally ran away. (Gen. 16:1- 6)

I know some of you are probably thinking, "First of all, I'm not about to give my man to anybody else! Shooooot, that was the craziest thing Sarai could've done!" But how many know that we've *all* done or said something, thought about it afterward and wondered, *Why did I do/say that?* It's not hard to see why Sarai went to this measure to give her husband an heir. She must have really wanted to help that prophecy along! If we're honest with ourselves, we'd see that we all, at some time or another, have tried to help God along in His work. Why? Because we felt that He either wasn't going to do what He said after all, or that He was just taking entirely too long to manifest His promise. I believe Ms. Sarai was thinking along these lines.

I also believe that Mr. Abram had been thinking the same way, due to how easily he went along with his wife's proposal. After all, 10 years had passed since the promise God had made him in the previous chapter ... and clearly, his wife wasn't bearing him an heir. So, this had to be the way, right?

We can put ourselves in their shoes right here — well, I sure can! Just think about it. God, in some way or another, has made you a promise. But 10 or more years have passed, and here comes an opportunity to fast-forward your way to that promise. And you think it's God. After all, God didn't specify how Abram would have an heir; he just said that Abram would have an heir! So, why not this way? I know I've made countless mistakes assuming this or that about the way God would fulfill a promise He'd made instead of simply trusting Him, asking Him to work patience in me, and doing His work as I wait. So, you see, it's really not that hard to relate to the matters of Sarai's heart or Abram's.

But God always has a more excellent way of doing things. The way Sarai and Abram chose clearly brought unnecessary drama to their lives and household. But God was still gracious enough to bless Hagar. God could have said to Abram, "Since you tried to manifest My promise the way you saw fit, just forget about it," and left the situation like that. Even then, before Jesus came on the scene, God was giving out a little mercy.

Well, I have two more examples I would love to share with you from the New Testament.

God's permissive will: John the Baptist prepares the way

Ideally, you've ascertained by now that before God does anything, He prepares. From the beginning of time, He has observed, then moved. Before He created man in His image, He prepared a place for him to live and govern. So, it should be no surprise to see that He began things the same way in the New Testament.

I will give you a few Scriptures here (still from the NLT). You're more than welcome to do some additional reading and research on your own.

> **In those days John the Baptist came to the Judean wilderness and began preaching. His message was, "Repent of your sins and turn to God, for the Kingdom of Heaven is near." The prophet Isaiah was speaking about John when he said. "He is a voice shouting in the wilderness, 'Prepare the way for the Lord's coming! Clear the road for him!' "** (Matthew 3:1-3)

Now, what I love about this particular passage is that it shows how God had fulfilled His promise to Abram back in the day regarding his descendants. Jesus came to us through this bloodline.

So now you have John the Baptist on the scene, trying to prepare the people for the Kingdom of Heaven — which would bring life more abundant — by repenting of their sins. In Verses 8-9, John the Baptist also warns the Pharisees and Sadducees, the self-righteous muckety-mucks of that day and time, not think of themselves as more than they were just because of their bloodline:

> **"Prove by the way you live that you have repented of your sins and turned to God. Don't just say to each other, 'We're safe, for we are descendants of Abraham.' That means nothing, for I tell you, God can create children of Abraham from these very stones."**

The message for us today: Don't get it twisted. Just because you've been in church all your life doesn't mean things are right between you and God. It's going to take sincere repentance and relationship cultivation efforts on your part.

In this passage, God is clearly sending a message to prepare the people's minds and hearts for the things that are to come. God's perfect will for us involves preparing us for our journeys, never leaving us ignorant of anything. (If we are ignorant, it's because we've chosen to be.) Then he gives us instructions to carry out.

The first assignment that Jesus had to carry out was God's perfect will concerning the people: that they be brought to the point of true repentance, rather than repentance through blood sacrifice. In other words, it was time out for failing to take responsibilities for one's sinful actions. (Even in the Old Testament — 1 Samuel 15 — the prophet Samuel pointed out to a disobedient King Saul that obedience was better than sacrifice.)

The ministry of Jesus finally begins in Matthew 4:12-17:

> **When Jesus heard that John had been arrested, he left Judea and returned to Galilee. He went first to Nazareth, then left there and moved to Capernaum, beside the Sea of Galilee, in the region of Zebulun and Naphtali. This fulfilled what God said through the prophet Isaiah: "In the land Zebulun and of Naphtali, beside the sea, beyond the Jordan River, in**

Galilee where so many Gentiles live, the people who sat in darkness have seen a great light. And for those who lived in the land where death casts its shadow, a light has shined." From then on Jesus began to preach, "Repent of your sins and turn to God, for the Kingdom of Heaven is near."

See, God already knew the lifestyles His people would lead. Go back thousands of years, when God was talking with Abram/Abraham. God told him how many years He was going to allow his descendants to live enslaved. He also told Abram that He would send someone to free those descendants. God fulfilled that promise through Moses. But that didn't go well either, because the Israelites remained in bondage of the mind. Now here comes John the Baptist preparing the way for the real Savior. And with Jesus comes real freedom for those who would receive Him!

The next instance of God's perfect will, found in Matthew 22:34-40, is seen in His most important commandment. Jesus had just shut down a group of Sadducees who tried to trip Him up with a question that involved resurrection from the dead, which they didn't believe in.

> But when the Pharisees heard that he had silenced the Sadducees with his reply, they met together to question him again. One of them, an expert in religious law, tried to trap him with this question: "Teacher, which is the most important commandment in the law of Moses?" Jesus replied, " 'You

must love the Lord your God with all your heart, all your soul, and all your mind.' This is the first and greatest commandment. A second is equally important: 'Love your neighbor as yourself.' The entire law and all the demands of the prophets are based on these two commandments."

Jesus knew exactly how to deal with the Pharisees. They had no choice but to be silent after that. It's the same when the enemy comes at us. When we use the Word – not our own words — to fight him, the enemy has to flee. Why? I'm glad you asked. In the beginning, God used words to speak things into existence. It's the same for those of us: When we use words, whether negative or positive, things happen. Proverbs 18:21 shows us that *"death and Life are in the power of the tongue: and they that love it shall eat the fruit thereof"* (KJV). When we begin to follow Jesus' lead and speak accordingly to the Word of God, we'll see a shift for the better in any negative situation.

Now here's two instances of God's permissive will in the New Testament:

> **When Jesus had finished saying these things, he left Galilee and went down to the region of Judea east of the Jordan River. Large crowds followed him there, and he healed their sick. Some Pharisees came and tried to trap him with this question: "Should a man be allowed to divorce his wife for just any reason?"**

"Haven't you read the scriptures?" Jesus replied. "They record that from the beginning God made them male and female." And he said, "This explains why a man leaves his father and mother and is joined to his wife, and the two are united into one. Since they are no longer two but one, let no one split apart what God has joined together." "Then why did Moses say in the law that a man could give his wife a written notice of divorce and send her away?" they asked. Jesus replied, "Moses permitted divorce only as a concession to your hard hearts, but it was not what God had originally intended. And I tell you this, whoever divorces his wife and marries someone else commits adultery — unless his wife has been unfaithful." Jesus' disciples then said to him, "If this is the case, it is better not to marry!" "Not everyone can accept this statement," Jesus said. "Only those whom God helps. Some are born as eunuchs, some have been made eunuchs by others, and some choose not to marry for the sake of the Kingdom of Heaven. Let anyone accept this who can." Matthew 19:1-12)

If you pay attention to what is taking place in these verses, you see God's permissive will coming into play concerning marriage. I've found these verses to be very interesting, considering that I've been married multiple times. God clearly is against divorce and never intended for His people to go through it. But I'm so grateful for His permissive concerning divorce. I don't believe that God personally wants men or women to stay in abusive marriages. God wants us all to be at peace. Thank You again, Jesus!

To grow in God and stay aligned with His perfect will, remember that a relationship with Him is a must. **DON'T LET THE ENEMY/INNERME KILL YOU OFF!**

Prayers for God's perfect will to be done in your life

Dear Father,

As I sit here contemplating my next move, I finally realize that I need You in my life. I can't make it without You. For so long, I really thought I could. In my head, I was the one making things move for me, not knowing that if anything good was happening for me, it was because of Your sweet grace and mercy. Father God, please forgive me for how foolish I have been! Help me from this day forward. Holy Spirit, I give You full permission to oversee my life. Guide me, as only You know how. God, please help me to walk out Your perfect will for my life. I'm so tired of just settling for Your permissive will. I'm ready for Your perfect will. It's in Jesus Christ's mighty Name I ask these things, Father God. Thank You for answering my prayer. AMEN.

Dear Father,

Thank You for this beautiful day that You've allowed me to see. Someone didn't make it, yet You saw fit for my family members and me to be here still. I just want to personally thank You for Your grace and mercy. Help my family members who are lost and don't know You as I am learning to know You. Help them to also see that You have need of them, too. Open their eyes of understanding as to why it's so important that we begin to walk in Your perfect will for our lives, and not continue choosing our own way of doing things. Help us all to remember that being on Your side doesn't mean we won't suffer, but You are always a very present help in our times of trouble. Thank You for answering every prayer, whether that answer is Yes, No or Wait. In Jesus Christ's mighty Name I pray, AMEN.

Dear Father,

Thank You for loving me throughout my life. Thank You for helping me daily. I need You every second. Thank You for answering my prayers concerning Your perfect will for my life! Thank You for providing. Thank You for supplying all my needs according to Your riches in Glory. Thank You for Your unmerited favor, which rests on my life and the lives of those who are connected to me. I thank You with all that's within my heart. I know that I'm not perfect. Help me to continue to strive to be the best that You have designed me to be. Help me to obey You and maintain total faith in Your perfect will for my life. In Jesus Christ's mighty Name I ask this. AMEN!

Dear Father,

Thank You for this beautiful day. Thank You for health and for a mind to serve. Lord God, help us to be about Your business daily! Help us, by Your Holy Spirit, to repent daily and obey You when You speak to us. Thank You for Your peace, Your love, and Your Joy! Fill us daily with what we need to walk out Your perfect will concerning us. Keep our minds. Help us to not become bewitched by the enemy's plan. You are the Author and the Finisher of our faith.

Thank You for the measure of faith You've given me personally. Help me to put it to use daily. In Jesus Christ's mighty Name I pray, AMEN!

CHAPTER TEN

Trusting God: The Payoff

*A*s I stated in my introduction, God wants us to grow daily in Him, trusting Him. Genesis 2, Verse 4, says that *"These are the generations of the heavens and of the earth when they were created, in the day that the Lord God made the earth and the heavens"* (KJV). The "4" represented by the number of this verse seems to correspond with the fourth day of creation, when God brought forth the lights in the sky to set the physical earth in motion (Genesis 1:14-19). These Scriptures deal with our "being," laying out our connection — mind, body and spirit — with God, our solid foundation and our safety/security.

Have you ever thought about this? The writers of God's Word often mention trusting Him. When you think about it ... why *not* trust Him? He is God. He created the heavens, the earth — and us! It's not because of man and woman "doing the do" that we exist. We exist because His Word states that He has need of us:

> **But you ... are a chosen people. You are royal priests, a holy nation, God's very own possession. As a re-**

sult, you can show others the goodness of God, for he called you out of the darkness into his wonderful light. (1 Peter 2:9, NLT)

Even before he made the world, God loved us and chose us in Christ to be holy and without fault in his eyes. God decided in advance to adopt us into his own family by bringing us to himself through Jesus Christ. This is what he wanted to do, and it gave him great pleasure. (Ephesians 1:4-5, NLT)

I truly believe God created the heavens and earth with us in mind. I tell you what — I'LL TRUST HIM! No matter how nervous or scared the things of this world make me, I choose to trust God with my life as well as those of my children, grandchildren and all who are connected to me. As He walks me through the valleys of the shadow of death, I will fear no evil. (Psalm 23:4). Daily He shows me more of Himself so that I may learn to trust Him with all that concerns me.

God's not asking any of us to be perfect. He sent His dearly beloved Son, Jesus Christ, to die on the cross so that we may be made perfect by faith in Him. So, stop your stinkin' thinkin' right now and allow the love of Christ Jesus to reveal why you should trust in a God you can't see physically. If you would allow this, I promise you'll be able to see God clearly. The Word shows us that the only way to the Father is through His Son (John 14:6).

I thought I knew God, but it wasn't until I became involved in a love relationship with Christ Jesus that I finally got a chance to meet and fellowship with God ... a God I've never seen; a God Who is such a gentleman that He waited for me to come to myself and fall in love with His Son in order to fall in love with Him. Mind you, God was already in love with me first. For various reasons I never allowed myself to experience it.

Giving myself over to God was the best decision I've made in my life! I urge you to give Him a chance with your life. What could go wrong? If you are honest with yourself, you'll probably have to admit that you haven't done that well on your own, no matter how much in control you think you are. Chances are there's a void in your life that you simply have not been able to fill, despite your strength of will, despite your persistence, despite your connections. That void can only be filled by the One Who created you ... whether you want to accept that or not.

Learn to trust God with all your heart. You've already tried the world's ways. You put your trust in your job — and, to use today's slang, it was a fail. You put your trust in family and friends — fail. You put your trust in romantic relationships – *epic* fail! The list can go on ... you get the point. Oh, I dare not leave this out: How many times have you tried to make things happen on your own? Think of that time you couldn't make ends meet. That bill was due; that shutoff notice threatened. Why do you think your services weren't suspended? Let me answer this one for you: it was because of the protection of our beloved Father God! How did that that other bill get paid when you didn't have the money? Let me answer this one for you as well: our beloved Father God! Who blessed you to be able to get school clothes and supplies for your children, knowing you just spent your last on money on bills and gas? You got it, it was our beloved Father God!

I was this person 11 years ago. I actually thought that I was making things happen on my own strength or with my manipulation skills. Today I know better. I still make mistakes; yet I have an Advocate Who fights for me daily.

I know it's not easy to trust God, especially when you think you've been making things happen all by yourself. I'm reminded of Romans 8:34: that Jesus makes intercession for us, pleading our case with God. And when Jesus finished His work on earth and ascended into heaven, He didn't leave us orphaned. He left us with the best help ever: the Holy Spirit, the same Spirit to which you refer when you say, "*Something* told me that." Let me introduce you to Him. He's your helper. He's the teacher of all things Jesus has taught … and more. He is the Holy Spirit, not "something." Give Him the respect that's due Him!

Trusting in a God Who sees and knows all is the best thing you could ever do. It's like making the best investment deal ever — you are spiritually and naturally set for life! Don't knock Him until you've tasted and seen that the Lord is good (Psalm 34:8).

Last but not least, I'll repeat the Scripture stated in my introduction: *"Trust in the Lord with all thine heart; and lean not unto thine own understanding. In all thy ways acknowledge him, and he shall direct thy paths"* (Proverbs 3:5-6, KJV)

DON'T LET THE ENEMY/INNERME KILL YOU OFF!

Dear Father,

I'm so grateful to You for sharing with me the mysteries of You and Your Kingdom. Thank You for calling me Your friend. That means a lot to me. You said in Your Word that a man who has friends must show himself friendly. Becoming friends with You, the Holy Trio, has been the best decision I've made. Thank You for showing me that trusting You with my life is the greatest thing ever. I can talk to You about any and everything. I don't have to worry about my business being all over the street or the Internet, and ultimately in the hands of my enemies. Yet, when You need to get a message to me concerning something I've shared with You, You use the right source to confirm that You heard my heart's cry. In Jesus Christ's mighty Name, I thank You for showing me how to trust You daily. AMEN!

Dear Father,

Thank You for showing me that I can truly trust You. Thank You for placing in my life people to whom I can vent, and who I can trust to authentically pray for me. You are so awesome. You know that sometime along our journey, we're going to need a friend — a person to confide in. A person to talk to about our inner demons. A person who will not judge us, but rather listen to us and pray for and over us. You said that we are helpers one to another, but if we don't ask You to choose our confidants, we may end up in messy situations that could have been avoided. In Jesus Christ's nighty Name, I thank You for just being who You are. AMEN!

Dear Father,

Thank You for having my best interests at heart. Thank You for showing me that if I trust in You, believe in Your Word and obey Your commands, You will give me the desires of my heart. The thing is, I'm only interested in Your desires for me. I'm not saying that I don't have certain desires; I am saying I trust YOUR desires for my life. I know that I am not my own. I belong to You, Father. My soul loves You. In Jesus Christ's mighty Name, I thank You, Father God, for listening to my prayers and answering them. AMEN!

I pray that the things the Holy Spirit has given me to share with you have blessed you tremendously. I pray that you've learned something new and that I have lit a fire within you, a yearning to get back to the things of God ... things He has placed on your heart and mind. Always remember that you are a precious jewel unto the Lord, no matter what your past looks like; no matter what you may be dealing with now or will deal with in the future. God will ALWAYS love you. Stay focused and know that you can cast all your cares on God, for He cares for you!

BIBLIOGRAPHY

Can you help me understand God's perfect will versus His permissive will? (n.d.). Retrieved from https://bible.org/question/can-you-help-me-understand-gods-perfect-will-versus-his-permissive-will

www.ingramcontent.com/pod-product-compliance
Lightning Source LLC
Chambersburg PA
CBHW070504100426
42743CB00010B/1756